A Touch
of Sabotage

1940 – 1945

by
Jack Goyder

I would like to extend my sincere thanks to Geoffrey Dutton and to Peter and Voirrey Lee for all their advice and help with the proofs.

First published in 1992 by Boolarong Publications
12 Brookes Street, Bowen Hills, Brisbane, Qld. 4006

Copyright © Jack Goyder

National Library of Australia
Cataloguing-in-Publication data

Goyder, Jack, 1920-   .
    A touch of sabotage.

    ISBN 0 646 12468 4.

    1. Goyder, Jack, 1920-   . 2. Great Britain. Army — Biography.
    3. World War, 1939-1945 — Personal narratives, British.
    4. World War, 1939-1945 — Secret service — Europe.
    5. Sabotage — Europe. I. Title.

940.548641092

BOOLARONG PUBLICATIONS
12 Brookes Street, Bowen Hills, Brisbane, Qld. 4006
Design and phototypesetting by
Ocean Graphics Pty Ltd, Gold Coast, Qld.
Printed and bound by Watson Ferguson Company, Brisbane.

For my wife Alison
and my children
Mark and Marie
Mandy and Kylie

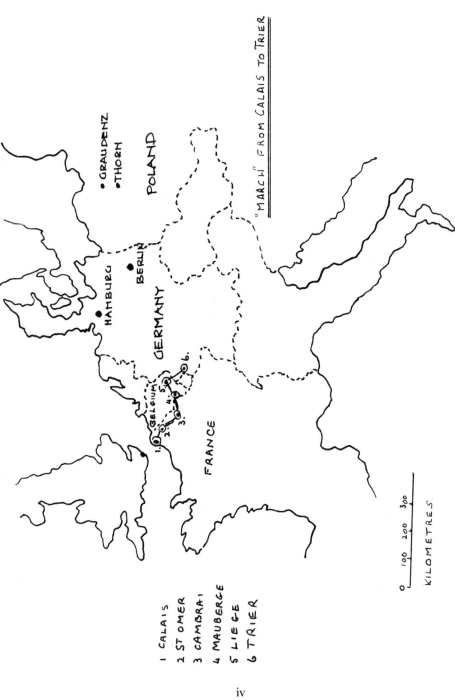

"MARCH" FROM CALAIS TO TRIER

GRAUDENZ
THORN
POLAND

HAMBURG
BERLIN
GERMANY

BELGIUM

FRANCE

1 CALAIS
2 ST OMER
3 CAMBRAI
4 MAUBERGE
5 LIEGE
6 TRIER

0   100   200   300

KILOMETRES

iv

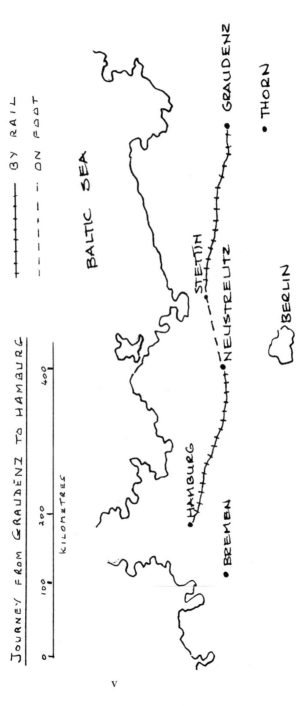

JOURNEY FROM GRAUDENZ TO HAMBURG

——————— BY RAIL
– – – – – ON FOOT

KILOMETRES
0   100   200   400

BALTIC SEA

BREMEN
HAMBURG
STETTIN
NEUSTRELITZ
GRAUDENZ
THORN
BERLIN
WARSAW

v

Contents

Jack Goyder, a doctor who lives in Queensland, was an 18-year-old soldier in the British Army when he signed on to work as a saboteur behind the lines. He could speak German and French.

Nearly five years later, he was flown back to England from Germany at the end of the European war. He had helped the Polish and French underground to blow up bridges, railways and even a concentration camp, as well as commit innumerable acts of sabotage; he had survived interrogations by the Gestapo and a number of hair-raising escapes.

Goyder tells his story without any fuss, which makes it all the stronger. Perhaps what comes through most compellingly is the wonderful resilience of youth, the ability to keep going through hunger, disease, brutality and loneliness.

Modest and humorous, A TOUCH OF SABOTAGE is compulsively readable.

Geoffrey Dutton

Chapter 1

May 1940

"You are now capable of carrying out individual subversive activity in enemy territory. It is your duty to sabotage the enemy's war effort in every way possible, both civilian and military, along the lines your instructors have trained you.

"You will be inserted into enemy occupied territory by becoming a prisoner of war; being fingerprinted as such, possibly photographed, and issued with a prisoner of war identity disk marked with your prisoner of war number.

"This is vital for your survival, that you should at all times be a British Army prisoner of war, and, if apprehended, your disk and number might just save your life.

"Finally you are on your own: trust no one at all. Good luck and God bless you!"

Such was the final stage of what had been a very brief but intensive period of training: an Army instruction course in almost everything that was contrary to the British idea of fair play. Indeed, it could have been called a course of unfair play in which one achieved an objective by the most devious and unexpected way possible; a veritable Marxist idea that the end justified the means; and it had all started because, during a lecture on foreign affairs by an officer in the Intelligence

Corps, I had been naive enough to volunteer that I could speak a couple of foreign languages.

At the time he noted my name, but I promptly forgot all about it until the day I was ordered to report with all my kit to the guardhouse, where a truck was waiting.

We had spent a very uncomfortable Christmas in oast houses at a Kentish hop farm; and since oast houses are constructed to dry hops by means of a good circulation of air (which most people call draughts) and since we had had such a freezing winter, everyone was getting a bit fed up with our situation, both with the lack of progress of hostilities and with the apparently pointless routine of barrack life; so I was overjoyed that something had occurred to break the monotony.

I got into the back of the truck, which was completely enclosed so that I could not see where I was going.

There were three other soldiers in the back, and we were driven to a house about three-quarters of an hour's drive from the camp, somewhere in Kent, but I had no idea of the route taken.

When we got down from the truck we were in front of a large country house surrounded by very extensive grounds, with tall oak and chestnut trees, large well-mown lawns and flower beds.

I was conducted upstairs to a room that had been stripped bare of furniture, and now contained two army 'biscuits' and two blankets. Each 'biscuit' was a one yard square quilted mattress, stuffed with a filling that was as hard as horse- hair, about four inches thick, which, when placed end to end with its twin, could be covered with a blanket tucked in to make a bed, then covered with the second blanket.

In the cold weather we had at this time, it was customary to sleep with one's greatcoat on top of the blankets and wearing army issue 'long johns', woollen socks and singlet.

I was provided with two sets each of PT shorts and battledress trousers and blouses, and had to wear these in place of my uniform.

The trousers were carefully folded in a sharp crease which was achieved and maintained by running a coating of Sunlight soap along the inside of the crease, then placing the garment under the bottom blanket on top of the mattress so that, after a night's sleep, the trousers were neatly pressed.

There were about ten of us on the course but I only knew one who was in my company, the others being total strangers, and we were discouraged from the start from talking about ourselves.

The one I knew in this special training course, Jim Clements, had joined the Territorial Army on the same day as I had, in 1938, two days after my eighteenth birthday; and we had kept together as much as possible from the start.

The first week was devoted to physical activity: exercises, running, jumping and armed and unarmed combat.

We learned that the heel of the hand is more effective than a fist; that stiff fingers jabbed into the throat could fracture the larynx and silently choke an adversary; that the edge of the hand was a useful weapon if applied to the correct spot, such as under the nose or against the carotid artery in the neck.

We were taught to apply the Japanese headlock and to break the neck by tightening the lock suddenly; that two hands, one over each ear of an opponent, could break his neck if suddenly jerked sideways and round.

We had not realized just how lethal an ordinary ballpoint pen could be if applied to the right places, eye sockets, under the ear, or behind the collarbone.

We had knife-throwing competitions, which were very popular, where we were shown how to throw a knife accurately and with sufficient force to penetrate deeply.

We were shown how to fire handguns without aiming along the sights and how to distract someone so as to gain an advantage, and how to lie convincingly.

The second week was spent doing all the above things plus map-reading and German speaking. We actually had a German soldier who had been captured early on in the war and who had volunteered to teach us colloquial German and idioms and phrases in daily use among the more lowly types of labourers and peasants. We were concerned with speech only and not with the written word.

The third week repeated all of the above plus a crash course in explosive devices and fuses, booby traps, how to avoid them and how to set them. This included talks on bridge construction and key elements in buildings, wiring detonators, how to avoid leaving behind obvious traces of wires; I was shown how to pick locks and padlocks, and how to recognize a lock that was difficult or impossible to pick without special instruments.

There were a number of other useful facts that had to be stored in the back of my mind.

When I had been at Grammar School every pupil had to learn eight lines of verse or prose every single day and write it out under the watchful eye of the form master. We were punished if we did not know it by heart, so it was, at the time, accepted as one of the necessary evils of school life.

The cumulative effect over the years was dramatic, in that we learned an enormous quantity of poems, plays and quotations, from Chaucerian English to French verse, large chunks of Shakespeare and many of the works of recognized poets. The benefit of all this was only appreciated after we left school and came across so many familiar excerpts from literature. This now became a great asset in giving me the facility of remembering almost everything taught on this course.

I was there for six weeks and at the end of this period we were assembled together and given various forms to sign, concerned, so we were told, with the Official Secrets Act.

We were also told of the penalties for divulging information relating to the course, the instructors or the location of the house, and we were warned that it was in our own interest to forget everything except the subject matter of the course.

As far as anyone was concerned, we were on a physical training and map-reading course.

Then followed the final talk and we were returned to our units in the closed truck.

It was now about the middle of May 1940, and all sorts of rumours were flying around about a German breakthrough in Belgium and the collapse of the supposedly invincible Maginot Line.

The French soldiers who manned this concrete defence line along the eastern borders of France, with its enormous guns, had a gold-coloured badge which bore the words *'On ne passe pas'*, which loosely translated means 'nobody shall get past us'. It seems that no one had thought that the German panzers would simply go round the end of the line to the north, via Belgium and the Netherlands.

It seems probable, in hindsight, that British Intelligence indicated that a collapse of the Allied armies in Europe was a distinct possibility and that a controlled withdrawal across the Channel would be necessary.

Furthermore, it was evidently decided that our battalion would form part of the rearguard action, should this eventuate.

It probably happened much more quickly than had been expected and, thus, we found ourselves literally thrown into the breech.

On May 20th 1940 my battalion left Dover in an old ferryboat, called the 'Canterbury', which had been plying the cross-channel trade for many years, and was big enough to accommodate our whole battalion.

The trip was only twenty odd miles but I was only nineteen years old and had never been outside England, and I was very excited about the thought of actually coming to grips with the Germans.

I was also one of the very few who knew that we and a few other units would be fighting a rearguard action in what was already a lost cause. I could have answered the question as to why the British Army's first motorcycle battalion had abandoned its role and left all our machines in England, had I not been scared stiff by the penalties of contravening the Official Secrets Act.

All our Norton 650 cc motorcycle combinations with sidecar drive and Bren mountings, all the B.S.A. 500 cc solo machines, the Daimler scout cars and the Bedford trucks had been left at the hop farm in Kent.

We were now just a plain light infantry battalion equipped with a minimum of small arms, anti-tank rifles and grenades.

The weather was exceptionally fine and warm, the sea as flat as a millpond, and the French coast was drawing closer so that what had been a smudge of shimmering grey on the horizon was now a definite coastline with pale green low hills beyond the beaches.

There was even the comforting presence of a solitary British fighter plane overhead.

Soon the ferry was pushing in to the docking area with derricks and railway sidings, and it was not long before we were disembarking and forming up on the dockside under the rather bored eyes of a few French dockside workers.

We marched out of the immediate dock area, across a few railway tracks, and took up positions around the dock perimeter.

I and two others had a Bren gun mounted on an anti-aircraft tripod, causing great amusement to the Frenchmen nearby who were manning a light anti-aircraft gun, huge by comparison with our little machine-gun. We were only about twenty yards away from them and they came over to shake hands and to give us some cotton wool to stuff in our ears. They said that the noise of their gun was horrendous and they had little doubt that they would shoot down the first German plane to show itself, adding that they thought our little gun would be too small to do any damage.

We secretly agreed with them but said that they would probably shoot down the British fighter plane overhead by mistake, but when we all looked up there was no sign of any aircraft at all, so we assumed that the plane we had seen whilst on board the 'Canterbury' had departed, and, since the 'Canterbury' herself was now just a speck on the horizon, it was reasonable to expect that the plane had stayed with the ship.

Nothing much happened for the next few hours except that we had our field rations brought to us and compared them with those of the French soldiers.

We had a packet each of very hard biscuits, known as hard tack, each biscuit about two inches square and packed in sixes in grease-proof paper; a tin each of Libby's corned beef, which was a particular favourite of mine, and an apple.

I was quite happy eating that sort of food and drinking water from my water bottle, and tea of the army variety, strong and sweet with condensed milk added.

The Frenchmen had a baguette or two apiece, the long thin loaf being split down the middle and spread with some sort of meat paste which was flavoured strongly with garlic; this put me right off it from the start and also made me very disinclined to carry on a close conversation with the French soldiers, who emitted successive waves of garlic breath with each sentence, further accentuated by their determined sense of bonhomie which made them put hands on my shoulder and speak with their mouths about six inches from my face.

They had water bottles full of red wine which was dry and rather harsh to the palate but quite pleasant after a few mouthfuls.

We were sitting down comfortably on the grassy bank chatting away, enjoying the warm sun and gazing idly out to sea as the 'Canterbury' reappeared on the horizon and slowly grew in size.

Another batch of troops, we concluded, on the way to join our happy little holiday jaunt.

At that moment the air-raid sirens all around us started to wail, and we jumped up to man our poor pathetic little Bren gun and started traversing the weapon back and forth looking for planes to shoot down.

The Frenchmen next to us were doing the same except that they had a seat and a handle to move the gun round and were swinging it energetically in all directions . . .

We didn't have long to wait for action.

There was suddenly a bright yellow flash in the sky, over the 'Canterbury', like a mirror briefly reflecting in the sun, and, to our horror, we saw the escort plane go down in flames into the sea.

We could still see no enemy planes and the 'Canterbury' was about three miles off the coast and proceeding unimpeded.

Then we heard a series of whining screams building up in intensity, louder and louder, until the sound was almost painful, and a large number of Stukas came belting down from the sky, with the sun behind them, appearing to be diving straight on to our position.

We were able to get a few wild bursts from the Bren gun, but it was impossible to see whether we had done any damage, and when we looked round to see how the Frenchmen were faring, we just saw the deserted gun and no sign of the soldiers.

Apparently they had decided that they were safer in their air-raid shelter, as, indeed, they were, because the planes were dropping a few bombs that exploded too near for comfort.

But the Stukas were evidently concentrating on the 'Canterbury'; we could see that she was the main target and had already been hit because she was burning at the stern, and it looked as though she had her life boats slung out on the davits, trying to launch them while the bombs were being dropped all around her.

Just when it looked as if she would make it to the shore there was an almighty explosion and the whole ship was obscured by thick black smoke and at the same time we could hear the Stukas flying off with a diminishing whine that was like the sound of the retreat of a swarm of bees.

In a moment or two the French soldiers were back at their gun, firing round after round at the retreating planes.

When the smoke cleared, after about ten minutes, we could see nothing of the 'Canterbury'. It was as if the ship had been wiped off the surface of the sea, and we realized then that it had been sunk, probably with most of those on board, although a few orange rafts were floating around with people clinging on to them; and some small craft were making their way from the harbour to pick up some of the survivors.

Shortly after this, we were withdrawn from the dockside and marched through the town and out to the surrounding countryside, which was mostly sand dunes and small isolated farms.

Our platoon was deployed in a section of perimeter extending from a railway track on the left, across a rather sandy green field for a distance of about a mile, to a small road on the right, beyond which there was a farm, called the *Ferme Trouille,* where we were able to get some rest and wash beside the pump and generally make ourselves at home in the large straw barn.

In front of our line the field extended for about half a mile, where there was a low ridge, grass covered, extending from the railway line to the road, possibly to mark the boundary of the farm and maybe to prevent flooding, although the latter was unlikely, because, in the middle of this artificial rampart, there was a farm gate, made of iron, hung on two brick piers about eight feet apart.

Such details become impressed on the mind when one spends many hours just looking in one direction and expecting a German tank to come bursting through the gap.

So intense was my concentration on this gate that I regarded it as my own special bit of France and vaguely wondered whether the Germans would have the decency to send one of their numbers out of the tank to open the gate before passing through, and, of course, politely closing the gate after they had passed through.

This little fantasy was cut short the next morning when we were ordered to dig ourselves in to the position. This entailed digging foxholes about five yards apart; roughly a cubic yard of the sandy soil was removed and piled behind the hole and at the sides, deep enough to allow one to stand comfortably and fire rifle, Bren or, in my case, a Boyes anti-tank rifle.

Jim Clements was now in the foxhole next to me, a burly young man, shortish, with fair curly hair, a fresh complexion and a usually smiling face which at present was set in concentration while he traversed his Bren gun trying to get a field of fire along the horizon and also into the air in case of air attack.

I was similarly engaged with my Boyes anti-tank rifle which was a diabolical weapon like a large heavy rifle about five foot long, with a bolt action and firing an armour-piercing bullet about four and a half inches long and twice the diameter of a .303 round. The rifle had a recoil-reducing muzzle and a recoil-reducing butt pad, but the recoil was still enormous, about three times the kick of a twelve-bore shotgun firing buckshot, and many types of tough guys on the firing range had tried to fire it without the recoil-reducing muzzle and had ended up with broken ribs or collar-bones.

I had fired it a few times on the range at a target but never at a tank, so I was a bit concerned that the tank it was meant to pierce might beat me to the punch, so to speak.

The traffic passing by the farm was really disproportionately dense for that small road, and it was all going in the same direction towards the docks.

There were trucks with weary-looking French troops wearing all types of unusual uniforms, from leather jackets and tank helmets to forage caps with bright piping and baggy trousers, some with greatcoats which had seamless ragged edges and could be buttoned back to allow free leg movement.

There were also African Somalis, identified for us by the farmer, tall fierce-looking natives with thick strange hair arrangements.

Mostly, however, there were the civilian refugees, usually on foot, trudging along, often with their most valuable possessions piled high on rickety farm carts, drawn by incredibly thin nags. Most of these had elderly people perched up on the piles of household goods. Some were pushing hand-barrows or old perambulators with young children on top of the packages.

They all looked really dejected and brought home to us

very forcibly some of the sad aspects of war. Maybe they had heard and believed some of the horror stories of the advancing German army, mostly fictional, of rape, pillage, looting and murder. One thing was sure: they were not going to stay behind and find out; they had abandoned their homes and simply wanted to get away from the fighting.

But where would they go? There was just nowhere to go when they reached the coast, and all they were doing at the moment was blocking the roads and making troop withdrawal more difficult.

For our part, it was very pleasant to lounge in the foxhole, admiring the view, watching the people and enjoying the warm weather.

This was the life for me.

There was very little warning, just an increasing whine which rose to a huge screaming shriek as a squadron of Stukas descended upon us. Each plane seemed intent on putting a bomb right into my foxhole and the earth around erupted, shook and rattled and was filled with noise and dust and the ever pervasive, never to be forgotten, smell of cordite.

All I could do was to bury myself as deeply as possible in the lowest recesses of the foxhole and pray as I had never prayed before, striking bargains with the Almighty, promising Him that if He let me survive I would spend the rest of my days as a priest.

Each bomb caused further head-splitting noise and unbearable blast and shock. The screamers attached to the wings of the Stukas really were terrifying as they produced a Doppler effect by their almost vertical dives.

I found myself screwing up inside waiting as the scream changed to the whistle of the bomb and the thump and blast of the explosion was followed by a whistling and buzzing of the earth, stones and metal fragments of the bomb itself.

The bombardment went on for about five minutes which seemed like five hours, and I was convinced that everyone had been wiped out except me.

Finally the scream of the Stukas became a diminishing

whine and was gone.

There remained a dead silence, accentuated by the recent assault on the eardrums. Then voices started. A head poked out of a foxhole. Then another, and soon almost everyone was talking, mainly, I suspect, out of relief and surprise that they were unhurt and that so many had survived. Some had not.

The bloke on my left had been lifted out of his foxhole by a bomb blast and laid a few yards from mine, very dead and peaceful looking and covered with dust. We had been joking together just before the bombing. His name was John German.

About an hour after the Stuka raid the shells started to fall.

There would be a furra-furra sound if they went past us overhead, or else a tearing sound, rather like ripping a sheet of canvas, which would increase in intensity and then end in a crump type of explosion followed by a spattering of shrapnel and dirt.

Some of the boffins in England had put forward the theory that you only heard a shell if it was not coming directly at you. That the shell which was heading your way travelled faster than sound and so would reach you before the sound, and therefore you would never hear the one that killed you.

It sounded like a load of codswallop to me but I suppose anyone grasps at straws at a time like that.

As long as one kept one's head down, it was not too bad unless a shell landed nearby, when it became truly terrifying because it felt as if it had singled you out personally; the blast of the explosion shook everything up in your head, made your ears ring, buffeted you around and poured sand and muck into your ears, nostrils and mouth so that you almost choked and always with that unforgettable smell of the cordite.

The furra-furra tearing sound was sometimes punctuated by a mid-air explosion which we thought must be some kind of double fuse on the shell. In hindsight, it was probably an anti-aircraft gun depressed to fire horizontally.

The bombardment continued on and off for some hours

and then abruptly ceased. It was almost as if one had gone completely deaf after all the noise and vibration.

It was pure joy just to have the chance to take a clean breath of air and poke one's head out of the beloved foxhole; how absurd to become so attached to a hole in the ground, but when it has been responsible for preserving your life it is surprising with what reluctance you part from it.

The air was filled now with confused shouting and it became apparent that we had been ordered to withdraw.

There was an army truck backed towards us about fifty yards away, with a few blokes in the back frantically signalling us to get in.

I looked around and saw that everyone else had gone; then I pulled myself wearily and stiffly out of the foxhole.

As I did so, I felt something pluck at my haversack and looked round to see who was there. There was no one near me and I realized it was a bullet which had just missed me.

I ducked back into the foxhole and removed the bolt of the Boyes anti-tank rifle, sticking it hastily in my haversack, and leaving the weapon in the foxhole; then, with a rush that would have done credit to an Olympic sprinter, I hared after the truck, which was beginning to move away.

I just reached it as it was accelerating and hung onto the tailboard where I was pulled up by the others in the truck. We all lay flat on the floor as a hail of light machine gun fire swept the truck.

So far, I thought, we'd done precious little to defend our perimeter, and now we were speeding towards the town, along the coast road, dodging in and out of the many abandoned trucks and wagons by the roadside.

Suddenly the truck swerved and, running right off the road, it hit a bank and rolled over. The driver had been shot in the head and killed, but we were unable to see anyone nearby who could have fired the shot.

Looking back on this incident it was probable that a 'Fifth Columnist' had been responsible for this attack since the

German lines were some way back, and we were only half a mile or so from the outskirts of Calais.

These 'Fifth Columnists' were German agents who had been infiltrated as Frenchmen into the area under attack, to cause panic and to disorganize any resistance ahead of the incoming troops. They were used in the Spanish civil war with great success and there is little doubt that the Germans exploited this idea. It is also likely that there were at this time numbers of these agents already planted in England prior to the expected invasion.

With the loss of the truck we were forced to march back to the town, but we'd not been on the road for many minutes before a squadron of Stukas appeared. We very quickly scattered on the sand dunes on our left and spread out as much as possible, giving passable imitations of those little sand crabs that burrow into the sand and soon become invisible.

We were certainly spotted and I think two of the Stukas bombed us and strafed us with machine gun fire, but I was too busy making myself invisible to pay much attention.

Eventually we were left alone to make our weary way back to Calais.

As we reached the outskirts of Calais we made for the Citadel, which was a prominent landmark where we expected to find the bulk of the battalion.

On the way there were ample signs that the aerial bombardment had been effective. Apart from the damage to buildings and the smoking remains of vehicles, there were soldiers lying with their brains coming through their skulls, blown-off bits of limbs separated from their owners, dead soldiers and civilians everywhere with horrific wounds, intestines trailing in the open, covered in flies, some of the dead with no signs of wounds looking as if they were just resting by the roadside.

In retrospect I was amazed that I could look at all this without emotion and can only conclude that, in situations like this, the mind is capable of cutting off one's feelings.

We took up new positions in the town, not far from the Citadel, which bordered a canal where a number of houses situated along the banks provided suitable cover.

It was quite eerie to be going into someone's house which had been vacated in a hurry, with pictures and photographs still hanging on the wall, food on the table in the kitchen, and sometimes the family cat left behind. I think that, in most cases, the family had simply gone somewhere nearby where they could shelter from the bombs and would re-occupy their house as soon as order was restored.

One house had an occupant, an old Frenchman, with grizzled short grey hair, deeply creased face with deep brown eyes, with a rather portly figure. He was wearing coarse canvas trousers supported by braces, and a dark blue grubby shirt; he was bare-footed and was wearing a greasy blue cloth cap similar to those worn by engine-drivers.

He was sitting at a table in the kitchen with the inevitable Gauloise cigarette, burnt down to about an inch and a half, adhering to his lower lip and hissing occasionally as the spit trickled down to the lighted end; he was obviously slightly drunk.

*"Allez, mon brave, une fine maintenant. A bas les Boches, hein?"**

I sat down with him and took a swig from the bottle he offered.

Next moment I was nearly choking and my throat felt a great searing burn down to the stomach. I had thought it was wine that he had offered and had not really believed him when he said it was brandy. Looking at the bottle I saw that it was a fine old Napoleon brandy.

As the fires in my stomach subsided I took a few more cautious and more civilized sips from the bottle and this time I enjoyed the smoothness of the spirit and told him it was very good.

He insisted that I keep the bottle and he gave me another one for my friends. He showed me several more bottles of the

---

* *"Come on, young man, have a brandy now. Down with the Germans, eh?"*

15

brandy that he had on the floor and told me that he was going to drink them all before they fell into the hands of the Germans.

I managed to find room in my haversack for the bottles.

The haversack had contained a gas mask and canister, gas goggles and a little tin of soaplike consistency which had to be rubbed on the gas mask eyepieces to stop them misting over. In common with most of the troops I had long since discarded the gas mask as a useless encumbrance but had kept the haversack strapped in place across my chest. It was now full of packets of Chocolat Menier which a shop owner down the road had given me and as many packets of Gauloise cigarettes as I could fit in.

A little redistribution of the cigarette packets into my large thigh map pocket allowed me to accommodate the bottles on a temporary basis.

I now felt that I could withstand a siege, as far as food and 'medical comforts' were concerned, although my defence consisted only of my Webley service revolver and about two dozen extra rounds.

On the sand dunes I had been offered the chance of carrying around four primed grenades but had passed them by as being too cumbersome, the cigarettes and chocolate were much more sensible.

I noticed that there was a glut of champagne among the troops as well as the cognac; however they were all so hyped up that there seemed little chance of anyone getting drunk.

Mostly we spent our time at the end of the street, firing across the canal, where the Germans were appearing and disappearing spasmodically.

I was surprised how clearly we could see them and I suspect we shot quite a few of them that day.

The Stukas came over again in the evening, but we had plenty of cover and just went to ground whenever we heard them; they flew very low over the roof-tops but there was no way we could fire back at them.

We slept that night in fits and starts, two hours on watch

and two hours off, until the dawn broke on another warm sunny day.

There was no doubt that the Germans had consolidated their positions in the night. When we looked at the promontory opposite the end of our street we could see the Nazi flag flying from the tall flagpole where yesterday there had been a French tricolour. Now the swastika proclaimed to all Calais that the Germans had taken possession.

But not yet, we thought, because there were lots of streets still occupied by us, and we knew that the Citadel would be a tough proposition for the Germans.

"Heh, Tommy, vous voulez quelque chose à manger?" [1]

It was always good policy to be polite to the locals so I accepted the long baguette.

"Bonjour et merci, hein. Qu'est qu'il y a dedans?" [2]

I thanked him for the bread but couldn't stop myself from enquiring about the contents, remembering the awful garlic meat paste that the French soldiers had eaten earlier; was it only three days ago?

"Regardez-le, mon ami." [3]

So I had a look and was confronted by a whole fish whose eyes stared at me blearily in an accusing way. I hastily closed the baguette.

"Oh ho, très bon, merci beaucoup," I said enthusiastically, *"Et au revoir, il faut partir."* [4]

I didn't have to go at all but I did have to pretend that I had urgent military business in the cellar where we slept, and the old Frenchman went on his way happily, content that he had contributed significantly to the Alliance.

When out of sight I hastily presented the baguette to a garbage can and got stuck into my favourite hard tack and bully beef, accompanied by swigs of very old and special Napoleon brandy.

---

1. *"Hey, Tommy, would you like something to eat?"*
2. *"Good day, and thank you. What's inside it?"*
3. *"Take a look, my friend."*
4. *"Oh yes, very nice. Thank you very much, and goodbye because I have to go."*

By now it was extremely hazardous to venture any further than the end of the street. From there we could see the great gaping craters left by the Stuka bombs where the old cobblestones had been flung in all directions greatly extending the peripheral damage of the bomb; there were shattered shop windows and exposed insides of houses overlooking the square, but if we hung about too long the German snipers would start zeroing down onto us and quite a few of my friends had finished their army careers merely by hanging about and looking at the scenery.

The main square in Calais is dominated by a very tall and ornate clock tower and we had known for some time that the German Fifth Columnists had been using this tower as a means of sniping at any easy targets. We were not able to blast it out of existence because, for one thing, we had orders to leave it alone, and, for another, we did not possess the necessary fire power. So we just had to regard it as another hazard in our very uneven contest.

By now the Germans had established two-inch mortars across the canal from us and were lobbing their bombs neatly into the streets so that we had to take cover, knowing that their ground troops would be moving nearer.

During the lulls in the firing throughout that afternoon we had heard the distant growling of tanks, rising and falling but getting steadily louder as they got nearer.

We didn't know it at the time, but these were the famous K Division Panzer Group, the equivalent of our Guards Brigade, under the command of Guderian.

Our job was quite simply to delay the Germans for a day, if possible, to allow the evacuation of most of the British Expeditionary Force from Dunkirk. In the event we delayed the advance for three days from the fall of Boulogne on May 23rd, so that it was not until the 26th May that the panzers moved towards Dunkirk.

Most of these three days were spent in street fighting in the town itself, where the houses' construction was ideal for this sort of defence, with three and four-floor terraced buildings with cellars which had grilles opening at pavement level and which provided reasonably good fields of fire with maximum protection against light arms fire, mortars and grenades.

As dawn broke on the 26th May we found that four of us were pinned down in a cellar, with no way to get out and with devastating mortar fire on to the cobbled streets outside.

Our ammunition had run out and there was nowhere to go.

On the previous evening shots had been coming through the walls of the room above us and it seemed that the Germans either had portable anti-tank weapons or, more likely, they had captured some of our Boyes anti-tank rifles and were using them as sniping weapons, the armour-piercing rounds simply going straight through the brick walls.

There was now no water: the supply had been cut off. We had finished the cognac supplied by the French civilians. We could see occasional glimpses of the enemy at the ends of the street, only fifty yards away, and we knew that the time was rapidly approaching when a grenade was going to find its way through the grille into our basement.

So when a voice said, "British Tommies, you will throw out your weapons and come out with your hands raised," in a surprisingly cultured voice with little trace of accent, we were rather more relieved than terrified. We crawled out of the cellar and walked out of the house into the street one by one, with our hands raised above our heads, to be confronted by some of the biggest soldiers I think I have ever seen.

Chapter 2

May 1940

They were wearing field grey uniform waterproof greatcoats, belted and with leather equipment which consisted of two vertical straps coming from the belt to go over the shoulders to join in the middle of the back by a ring and a short extension strap to the back of the belt. The greatcoats reached down to about nine inches above the ground. They all wore thick soled slip-on top boots, *'Stiefels'*, in which a number had stick grenades pushed down the top of the boots.

They had large steel helmets, painted grey, covering the ears and flaring out at the back of the neck, and they had goggles pushed up onto the helmet.

They also carried *Schmeisser* machine pistols with slings suspending them from the neck.

More stick grenades were stuck into their belts.

They would all have been well over six feet tall and the bulky greatcoats made them look like giants.

They were altogether, a most impressive sight, although I couldn't help feeling that they must have been very hot inside those greatcoats in that warm summer weather.

We were marched to the large square in the centre of

Calais, overshadowed by the tall clock tower which had been used as an observation post, and later for sniping and was very lucky to be standing in one piece.

We were lined up in rows and searched briefly for weapons.

My gas mask haversack, slung in the approved fashion across my chest, was still filled with bars of French 'Chocolat Menier' and soon came under the scrutiny of the large blond young German searching me; I thought he was after the chocolate when he pulled out three bars held together by a large shining splinter of shrapnel which had ripped into the haversack quite unnoticed by me during the fighting. The German pulled out the splinter, replaced the chocolate in my haversack and, with a wide grin on his face, he took the piece of steel and held it just over my heart at the exact spot it had entered the haversack, shaking his head and acknowledging that I had had a very lucky escape. He then handed me back the piece of shrapnel saying 'souvenir'.

During this episode, more and more prisoners had been led into the square, so that there must have been about two or three hundred British troops.

The wounded were put on one side and the remainder were sorted out into a long line three abreast and marched out of Calais in a southerly direction.

The weather was really hot and we were battle-weary, smoke-grimed, filthy dirty, fairly hungry and also utterly dispirited at the obvious superiority of the German forces.

We had got very mixed up in the street fighting and there were groups from various British Regiments, including our own, the Queen Victoria's Rifles, also representatives of other regiments including RAOC, RASC, RAMC, Rifle Brigade, Welsh Guards, Argyle and Sutherland Highlanders and other groups from the 51st Highland Division, and a few other odds and ends. Then there were French Army and Navy groups, Belgians, Dutch and a few doubtful characters who wore French uniforms but were probably German infiltrators ordered to go along with us to pick up any useful talk.

We didn't really march: we just walked because we had to.

There were German guards with rifles every ten yards and they were very ready to shoot and did, in fact, shoot and kill one or two of the more adventurous souls who thought they could slip away and hide. Maybe some did get away but they would have been very few indeed. The troops we had guarding us were not front line troops but older, more tired and, for the most part, very bad-tempered. I suppose they had to be, because their officers were keeping a close eye on them and every time an officer came by the guards would start shouting, threatening and pushing us to hurry us along.

We walked on the right side of the road, constantly inhaling the diesel fumes from the trucks that poured towards the coast, heavily laden with guns and troops.

Those who were classified as 'walking wounded' were helped by the fit ones and the pace was a fairly slow walk.

A Scotsman walking ahead of me was certainly dawdling more than the others and when a guard prodded him in the back he turned round with a furiously malevolent look and said in a broad Glaswegian accent, "Awa' and piss in yer boots, you German bastard"! The guard dropped back a couple of paces in amazement, then recovered enough to shout a rather weak *"Los! Los!"*, looked over his shoulder to make sure no officer was near and then dropped back to march alongside me, still looking a bit apprehensively towards the Scot who was muttering under his breath.

It was noticeable that the German troops, going in the opposite direction, were marching along smartly, singing the most stirring and melodious songs that I have ever heard.

The German version of 'The Happy Wanderer' was one of these, and no choir could have rendered a better version of it, with tenors and baritones and basses all singing in harmony.

The German army rankers are specially trained to sing these marching songs which are considered an essential part of march discipline, and with Germany's racial background of music, the troops enter into the spirit of the singing so well that they devise point and counterpoint in the songs and the results are irresistible.

Nothing could be more moving or dramatic than to have melodious and stirring singing, clear voices, amidst the dust and grime of war, singing to the time of their marching feet.

One can so easily imagine that, at this time, the morale of the German army was at its height; and such singing expressed the confidence and contentment that these troops so obviously felt; in direct contrast to the feelings of uncertainty and bewilderment on our part as we seemed to be the losers, trudging along almost ashamed of ourselves.

But even at this, one of the lowest points in our experience, I don't think that we considered the possibility of losing the war.

The order is given by the Unterofficier who is the equivalent in rank to a sergeant, who shouts out the command:

"Fahren gegen England. Ein, zwei, drei, sing"

The troops respond with the following:

"Heute sollen wir ein Lied singen,
Und trinken schon roten Wein.

Und die Gläser sollen dabei klingen,
Weil es muss, es muss geschieden sein.

Gib mir deine Hand, deine weisse Hand.
Lebe wohl, mein Schatz, lebe wohl.

Lebe wohl, mein Schatz, lebe wohl,
Lebe wohl.

Wenn wir fahren, zwei drei vier,
Wenn wir fahahren, wenn wir fahren

Gegen England JA WOHL!!"

Translation of this song is roughly as follows:

Today we're going to sing a song
And drink good red wine.

And the glasses will clink together
Because we have to be parted soon.

Give me your hand, your white hand,
Let us live well, my sweetheart.

Soon we march, soon we march
Against England. Yes indeed!

After we had been trekking for about two hours the column was halted and we were allowed to rest by the side of the road.

The sounds of gunfire had pretty well subsided.

After an all too brief ten-minute rest we were prodded back on to the road and continued our march.

For two weeks we plodded on.

The French population watched us silently and sadly: a long winding column of tired, dirty and unshaven rabble with lacklustre eyes and all the spirit knocked out of us.

Sometimes an old lady would rush up to the column with a couple of loaves of bread, braving the anger and threats of the guards. Sometimes children would be instructed to hand us sandwiches or throw food towards us.

In some of the villages we passed through, the whole population turned out and often they organised a bucket of water with cups by the side, sometimes with a tablecloth, very French, so that we could go and help ourselves to a drink; and everywhere we went there were packets of sandwiches, either thrown towards us or handed to us by women and children.

Our particular column must have been about two miles long, so these good people must have depleted their food supplies considerably.

The names of the villages became meaningless after a while, but the general direction was south to St Omer, thence to Cambrai, then east to Mauberge and into southern Belgium, along the river road to Liege.

At night we were herded into a suitable field and the guards were posted all around it. The night guards travelled by truck to the next destination and were ready to get us sorted out at night whilst those guards who had marched with us got some sleep.

Sometimes, especially when a German officer was around, the guards would shove us around with the rifle butts, shouting *"Raus! Raus!"*; and, occasionally, they would roughly push the civilians away and threaten to shoot them, and generally make a show of efficient crowd control, but as soon as the officer had gone they returned to their normal state of tolerance.

What they did not tolerate, though, was anyone dropping out of the column for any reason at all. If anyone wanted to relieve themselves they had to wait for the ten-minute break in each hour, when we stopped and rested by the roadside. Any attempts to leave the column was met with shouts and blows from the rifle butts or the guards boots.

We helped along some of the lightly wounded and, if they were unable to continue, we would tell the guard during the break, and he would stay with the wounded man until the column had passed and put him on a truck that was bringing up the rear.

The guard did this very reluctantly, because it meant that he would have to march back to regain his place in the column, and most of the guards were as tired as we were by the end of the day.

By now it was early June and the weather continued hot and dry, which was fortunate, because we were sleeping in the open air at nights, just lying on the grass in the fields, and had no way of keeping warm other than by huddling together in groups. However, by the time the day was over, we were so footsore and weary that we just dropped off to sleep straight away.

As we filed into the field at the end of the day we were dished out with some thin vegetable soup, which we had to collect in any container we could lay hands on, from mess tins to ordinary old rusty tins or mugs picked up on the march. We were also given a loaf between four or five according to supplies, and this had to last us the whole of the next day. Needless to say, most people ate the whole lot in one session.

I was then very grateful for the chocolate which I carefully rationed day by day.

I was with some of my battalion but mostly men from other companies of the Queen Vics.

I had not seen Jim Clements since we were separated during the street fighting in Calais. It was only much later that I learned that he had been killed in the town.

There were some cases of guard brutality, probably where the particular guards had a real or fancied grudge against us, but for the most part they were fairly tolerant and the shouting and rifle butt blows were really to satisfy their superiors.

I believe that a number of prisoners were shot and killed trying to escape at night, just as I believe some did escape successfully.

There was no way that the guards could know, other than by counting us in the morning before moving off, and that was done in such a slipshod manner that they got a different number almost every time they counted.

For some unknown reason the guards always seemed to have difficulty with counting, and, instead of doing it as the prisoners passed a given point, like counting sheep, they always counted a column of four stretched for about a hundred personnel. This was made more difficult by the movements of some of the prisoners who could have been counted twice over.

After counting, the guards would have a hurried conference, no doubt settling among themselves which number to report, and then the senior among them, usually an Obergefreiter, or corporal, would march up to the Feldwebel, a sergeant-major, turn to face him, suddenly clap his extended fingers down the sides of his thighs, at the same time jerking his head up and his shoulders back and clicking his heels sharply, then in a very firm, loud and confident voice, no doubt to disperse his own doubts, would report the number present which the Feldwebel would write down in his notebook and then give the order to march.

Finally, about the ninth of June, we arrived at a camp on the road to Liège, probably about ten miles from the city,

It was nothing more than a huge field with barbed wire

round the perimeter, patrolled by guards, and with a wide gate which was the only entrance and exit.

Inside the barbed wire was another smaller fence, allowing a corridor of about eight feet wide all the way round. In this corridor was concertina barbed wire to make a trip through the wire very slow indeed so that the guards would have plenty of time to pick off their target.

We spent the night as usual sleeping on the grass, huddled together in groups, although the weather was still quite warm.

In the morning, before we marched off, all the Belgian soldiers were isolated from the rest of us, and put into trucks, which we were told would be going to Brussels, where these soldiers would be returned to civilian life in Belgium, because their country had surrendered to Germany and was therefore no longer at war.

Almost immediately we turned south in our march, and in about four days we reached the town of Trier, just east of Luxemburg.

The day before we had stopped earlier and I think the purpose was to get to Trier at a certain time when we would make the maximum impact on the German population.

It is quite possible that they were told that a large column of prisoners of war were being brought in to the prepared camp at Trier, and I believe that it was the intention of the German authorities, under the direction of the Minister for Propaganda, Herr Goebbels, to arrange a scenario where the German people could compare the rabble of the enemy with the clean brave front of the German troops.

Certainly as a propaganda move it was very effective.

As we approached the town of Trier it was noticeable that the German guards smartened themselves up considerably and became a bit more threatening in their attitude to drive us through the town.

It was also noticeable that some of the townspeople were not impressed by this propaganda and many just looked the other way. But the majority were certainly interested, especially the younger groups, and one could read from their expressions that now they knew they were going to win the war if this was the opposition.

At the centre of the town, in the large open cobblestoned square, we were halted to allow the stragglers to catch up.

From most of the windows there flew swastikas and also a large number of other flags, presumably local district flags which may have represented the old boroughs or coats of arms, because they looked ancient.

I had never seen so many window boxes filled with flowering plants, and I thought that Trier was altogether a very pleasant-looking town.

A squad of German soldiers, some thirty strong, came across the square, marching smartly to attention and singing one of their most rousing and popular marching songs.

We all had a feeling that such a scene could only have been contrived and the hands of that genius of propaganda, Dr Joseph Goebbels, was, in hindsight, fairly apparent.

We were, after all, the first really big batch of prisoners that the German civilian population had seen, and the Germans had had no real casualties in the war so far, so it must have been reassuring to the civilian population that their brave lads were not really at risk against a rabble like us.

Chapter 3

June 1940

The prisoner of war camp at Trier, although just a transit camp, was brand new and very well organized.

We were able to get back some of our self-respect by showering, shaving, washing our clothes, allowing our foot blisters to heal and generally smartening ourselves up.

Over the next few days we had a chance to regroup mentally and adjust to a totally new way of life where no-one was allowed to think for himself and where the future was bleak indeed. It was now the end of June and I realized that, for the first time in my life, I had passed my birthday without realizing it. So I was now twenty years old.

We were finally fingerprinted, photographed and interrogated.

The interrogation was very casual, there was no question of name, number and rank and no more. They did most of the talking and knew all about our units and even the names of our company commanders.

We were then each issued with a metal disc about two and a half inches long by one and a half inches wide with two holes for a cord so that it could be hung from the neck. It had perforations across the middle longways so that when the owner died one half stayed with the body and the other half could be sent to the central register to check the identity. The number was impressed on each half.

This was the expected Kriegsgefangenennummer (prisoner of war number) which was to be the means of saving my life on three separate occasions, although I didn't know this at the time, and I was certainly not fit to do any of the suggested tasks for which I had been so carefully trained. I would just have to get as fit as I could as soon as possible.

It was now July and the rumour in the Trier camp was that we would be shifted to a regular prisoner of war camp, probably in Poland.

The move seemed more imminent the next morning when we were all assembled on the central parade ground; two guards came along carrying a small platform which they placed in front of us. In due course a German officer appeared and mounted the rostrum.

He delivered his speech in moderately good English which contained phrases like 'for you the war is over' and 'if you obey orders you will be treated well according to the Geneva Convention' and 'you are expected to conduct yourselves as soldiers and obey all the orders from your guards' and 'you will be shot if you attempt to escape' and 'you will be home for Christmas' and sundry other appropriate phrases.

When he had finished he stepped down from the rostrum and left, having been saluted smartly by the Feldwebel, the sergeant-major in charge of the parade, who instructed the guards to count us in squads of a hundred at a time.

This counting took about a further hour because of the usual shuffling around of the prisoners, done mostly to annoy the Germans, necessitating recount after recount until at least two of the guards came up with the same figure which was then noted by the Feldwebel, who motioned to the guards to take us away.

Each group was marched in turn to a large barn-like building on one side of the compound.

We were told that they were delousing sheds, and, as we

were fairly heavily infested with straw lice, we were quite happy that something was being done to stop the interminable itch caused by these creatures.

As we went in, we had to take off all our clothes, tie them in a bundle with strips of cloth provided, and mark them with a label of the POW number. Our boots were tied together by the laces, similarly numbered but put in a different pile.

The clothes were then put into a sort of kiln and subjected to sufficient heat to kill the livestock without burning the clothes themselves, although in some cases the khaki battledresses were scorched a darker brown.

There were few fleas but scores of straw lice which are about the same size as a small flea but pale cream coloured and transparent, the blood they suck in colours their bellies a dark brown. They could be killed manually by squeezing them between one's fingernails or by running a very hot wire down the seams of the clothing, an area they seemed to prefer to live in and hatch out their eggs.

Having seen our clothes disappear into the kiln, we then passed one by one through a room where all our hair was cut off with electric clippers, including pubic hair, armpits and chest.

Next we proceeded into the showers, which were lukewarm at first and went cold after ten minutes which was the signal for us to get out of them.

We had each been provided with a cake of ersatz soap, which was a cross between pumice stone and household soap. We were told that it was a by-product of coal, and, whilst it did work, it was difficult to decide whether the effect was achieved by the scouring action of the soap or by the minimal lather it produced. The soap and towel were my first experience of the ingenuity of the German scientists in the field of ersatz goods.

The towel was like a drying up cloth in appearance but was made from straw.

Other examples which I encountered later were also produced from coal. These were 'Kunsthonig' (synthetic honey) and *'Kunstmargarine'* (synthetic margarine), sometimes labelled *'Tafelbutter'* (table butter) but tasting exactly the same as the margarine. We also had the famous ersatz coffee produced by drying, roasting and grinding up acorns.

By the time we had finished drying, our clothes had been sufficiently roasted, including the pocket contents, which were somewhat crinkly and shrunk bits of paper for the most part, and we were able to get dressed and to feel the luxury of wearing clothes without the accompanying itch and to feel actually clean again. This did a great deal of good to our self-respect which had taken a series of blows since we had left Calais, which seemed a hundred years ago but was only a little over a month.

Unfortunately we had little time to enjoy our new-found cleanliness because we were lined up outside the shed, and, much to our surprise and disgust, we started off out of the camp and, as we thought, back on to the march across Europe!

However, we went only as far as the railway station at Trier, where we were obviously expected because there was an extra detail of guards and a long train consisting almost entirely of cattle trucks, with a passenger coach hooked on to the tail end, and another behind the engine.

There were about fifteen cattle trucks in all. They were the matt reddish-brown of the French rolling stock and had stencilled on the sides that they could accommodate *'vingt hommes ou huit chevaux'*, twenty men or eight horses.

That's not too bad, we thought, twenty men to a truck will be luxury after all that marching.

We noticed that the normal one yard by nine inches opening at each end had been boarded up and heavily intertwined with barbed wire so that we could not see out.

A further pleasant surprise awaited us when we were dished out with a whole loaf of bread each and told to fill our water bottles with water for the journey. Nobody told us how long we would be in the truck and we assumed that we would be a day or so, four days at the most.

We also assumed that we would be let out at suitable

intervals to go to the toilets in the stations and that we would be able to replenish our water supply at that time.

The majority of us, therefore, conserved our loaf on that basis, although some scoffed the whole loaf in the first day.

The loaves were the official German army issue, known as the 'Kommisarbrot' and measured about eleven inches long by about five inches square and were a combination of rye, chaff and fine sawdust. When new, they could be sliced as thinly as one-eighth of an inch and were so dense that they did not crumble at this thickness. However, if they became stale, as they did after about five days, they developed deep fissures in the crumb part, could not be cut at all and it was possible to hammer a nail into wood with them.

When they reached this stage of hardness, they could be moistened in water and then chewed; however, after a week, they began to get a green mould on them which tasted revolting, and the bread inside the mould tasted very bitter. They could be and were eaten in this condition when one was starving.

We were now told to get into the trucks, but we found that sixty of us were crowded into each truck, which meant that we could not sit, let alone lie down.

As soon as sixty of us were in the truck the guards slammed the sliding door and secured it with a padlock.

It was at first rather dark in the truck, but soon our eyes adjusted and we could see a narrow slit of daylight through the boarded-up grille. We discussed what we should do about a toilet and decided that we would have to designate one corner to be used for all purposes, so we chose a corner that had a small crack in the floorboards and this was the toilet.

As we had supposed that the guards would let us out at suitable intervals, we were not too worried about people piddling in the corner.

There was a good deal of grumbling and growling, but by now the guards had left, presumably to travel in the passenger coaches at the front and rear of the train, so no amount of yelling and thumping made any difference. We just had to make the best of a very bad job.

We managed to get some order into our new residence by one man sitting with his back to the rear end of the truck and opening his legs to allow the next man to sit immediately in front of him facing in the same direction and repeating this arrangement until the last man in the row was up against the opposite wall of the truck.

By sitting thus in orderly rows half the men could have a sit down whilst the others stood. This at least gave us something to do and allowed a fair distribution of sitting and standing.

The journey was not too bad for the first few days, although the smell increased alarmingly as we had no outlet for toilet purposes and had to sacrifice some of our precious space in one corner to allow all the piles of faeces to accumulate.

Sixty men, half of them with diarrhoea, amass a surprising amount of waste product in four days, and by that time we were more than ready to be let out of the truck.

However, it soon became obvious that the German guards were keeping well away from our trucks in their relatively luxurious carriages, and had no intention of letting us out.

We were only making very slow progress because we were continually being shunted into sidings to allow other trains to pass.

By the end of a week we were in a very sorry state because we had consumed all our bread and most of our water and there was still no sign of the doors being opened.

Also by now some of the men were too weak and sick to stand and they were just lying down, hardly moving or protesting when someone stood on them.

In desperation some of those near the boarded up grille had managed to break away some of the boarding and were able to get a little more air into the truck.

We had tried repeatedly to pull up some of the floorboards, but we had no implements and they were too solid to move.

The whole damn truck was just too solidly built; walls and

roof and floor were all tried, even to the point of getting bruised and bleeding hands with the effort.

All we could do was to wait.

At the end of two weeks we could hardly have cared less whether the doors opened or not.

All of us had dysentery, passing mucous and streaky blood; some were unconscious, all were starving hungry and too weak to walk or to stand.

The stench was horrific but we were past caring.

I knew that some of us were dead but it was not until we stopped finally at Torun in Poland, and were allowed out onto the platform, that I realized that five of our number had died.

I think that the German guards themselves were a bit ashamed when they finally let us out. But it may have been due to the almighty smell that they gave us more or less the run of the station for at least four hours, during which time we cleaned up as much as possible with three taps and about eight hundred men, all with diarrhoea, most of which was bacillary dysentery, trying to drink the water in between washing themselves and going to the toilets.

The dead were removed by truck very soon after we disembarked so I have no idea how many in all died, but it would have been a few dozen.

The rest of us were formed up eventually and shambled along the cobblestones of this ancient Polish town, which possesses some fortresses and is situated on the river Vistula, really quite picturesque, except that we were in no condition to appreciate it, or think of anything except just putting one foot in front of the other.

We were once again just a rabble, stinking and slouching, with dirty, crumpled, stained uniforms, scratching away at the returned lice and generally presenting an unlovely picture.

However, this time the population was Polish, and very sympathetic towards us, to the extent that some of them, mostly the women, were willing to brave the anger of the guards, by throwing loaves and food to us as we passed along the streets. Some even applauded us, but most looked at us with great compassion and sorrow showing on their faces.

My impression of the Poles was that it was the womenfolk who stood up to the German oppression better than the men. This may have been caused by the great fear that the men had of the Germans, who regarded Poles as a race only slightly better than Jews, and, to the Germans, now well under the spell of Adolf Hitler's ideal of Aryan race purity, Jews were much lower than animals and were to be treated as such.

The Germans I spoke to, normal working class types, had the usual logical views about life in general, but, where the Jews were concerned, there was a blind spot, a complete humanity gap, which allowed them to say, and to believe, such things as 'Oh yes, but Jews are not human beings: they are a race of parasites which must be destroyed if we are to survive.' There was no way in the world that this idea could be wiped from the minds of Germans who had this doctrine instilled into them for at least the past generation, relentlessly and methodically.

It was quite apparent that the whole German nation, a race of brilliant minds and eminently logical thought, had been systematically brain-washed with this obsession about the Jews, so that they believed completely Hitler's tenets of Aryan faith, which held that the only solution to the contamination of the German people with Jews was to eliminate those Jews from the whole of Germany, by killing them.

This idea of genocide would, I am quite sure, have been extended to any countries subsequently conquered by the Germans, including Great Britain and the USSR.

So, whilst the Jews were to be exterminated, the Poles could and would be treated very badly indeed, at every opportunity, by the Germans, who looked upon them as the slaves of the Aryan race.

Later in the war, when the Russian prisoners started to arrive in Poland, they too were treated in a manner worse than might be expected with animals and, partly because the

USSR did not subscribe to the Geneva Convention, no particular care was taken to keep the Russian prisoners alive. They were fed if they worked but that was all.

In 1940 and 1941 it was the Poles who looked over their shoulders continually while talking to you.

In 1944 and 1945 it was a precaution adopted by the Germans themselves, particularly in the lower ranks of the army, which was at that time infiltrated by all types of fanatical Nazi Party members. In particular, there were members of the NSDAP, the National Sozialistiche Deutsches Arbeits Partei, who would shop their own mothers if they suspected that they were speaking out against Hitler, and who were able and willing to call down the Gestapo on anyone even vaguely suspected of subversive talk or activity.

We were taken into one of the large central fortresses in Torun, renamed Thorn by the Germans, who renamed a number of the towns in Poland which they found difficult to pronounce, or which had previously had Teutonic names.

This fortress had the number XVII on the entrance gate and was always referred to as Fort 17. It was a huge and imposing edifice which had a central parade ground larger than a football field, surrounded by the fort proper which was a honeycomb of passages and cells, all with low curved vaulted ceilings. There were about three storeys but the levels were split, so that there may, in places, have been four or five storeys. They were all connected by passages, and most had stout timber doors with large old-fashioned locks, of the type one can open with a bent nail.

Below the ground level there were dungeons with only slits for windows, which looked out on to the moat which, now dry, would have protected the fort effectively from invading armies.

There was ample room for three or four thousand prisoners, and this was the central fort and the headquarters of Stammlager XX, shortened to Stalag XX, and was mainly for army prisoners of war non-commissioned ranks.

Though mostly British, there were also Poles, French and a

few British Merchant Navy types who had been there for some months, probably captured in German ports at the beginning of the 'phoney' war from September 1939 to May 1940, when, although an official state of war existed, there was no real conflict.

Initially we were isolated from the inmates of Stalag XX until we had been through the now familiar routine of delousing, which took place in a separate building apart from the fort, about five minutes walk away.

Finally, when we were allowed into the fort, we were conducted to our sleeping space in a larger than usual part of the fort, consisting of a room about thirty yards by ten yards with a concrete floor and a ceiling about twelve feet high.

The space was filled with bunks which were newly built wooden erections, two tiers high, six foot two inches long and eight foot wide, intended to sleep four down and four up.

The sides of the bunk were six inch planking to stop those lying on the outside from rolling on to the floor, and the whole construction was of six inch pine planks with three by three posts supporting the upper bunk and raising the lower bunk twelve inches off the floor.

Three of these bunks stretched across the room, leaving a yard passageway on each side, and there were about ten rows of such bunks; thus about one hundred and eighty men slept in each room in the large halls, but there were numerous smaller rooms with correspondingly fewer bunks.

We were given hessian palliasses to fill with straw and we used our rolled up clothes as a pillow.

We had no change of clothing and were expected to wash everything each Sunday with an issue of two tablets of ersatz soap per week.

Washrooms and toilets were situated at the end of each corridor and were surprisingly well equipped with showers and hand basins and toilets which were made of scrubbed pine in decks of six along the walls, without any partitions, so that sociable conversation could proceed unimpeded.

German newspaper was provided on a shelf by the door, not for reading but to tear into neat squares for toilet purposes.

We had two parades in the square each day where we were assiduously and laboriously counted by heavily breathing peasant German guards who were probably products of the First World War and were now too old to fight (although their turn would come later when they were relentlessly sent to their deaths on the Russian front).

Most of them were good old rascals, not above swapping food for one's cherished possessions, like signet rings, cigarette cases, St Christopher medals, wrist watches and so on.

One has to remember that food was extremely short, and everyone was ravenous the whole time, so that the main topic of conversation centred round food and all the remembered and now deeply regretted times that one had thrown away unwanted food or left some uneaten meal. Constantly the boys were talking about exotic meals they had eaten which were often, in reality, everyday meals which had become glamourized by their absence.

There was still a lot of diarrhoea among the troops with frequent blood-stained stools, and this was a problem with the unavailability of drugs and the absence of suitable foods. It was the same bacillary dysentery as before that we all had, and this spread like wildfire around the fort; it was only the fitness of the troops initially that prevented a mass extermination by the disease, which is a serious possibility under any circumstance.

Probably the lack of food helped to cure the illness, because eventually we got rid of it and settled down to our captivity, which was very little different from that of army barrack life, with the constant chores of cleaning, parading, sleeping and eating, although the latter was a bit deficient.

The Germans insisted on two roll calls a day, one on rising, at about six am, and one at about four pm, although quite often they threw in another one in the middle of the day, for no apparent reason at all other than just to irritate us.

It was no joke to be on parade for an hour and a half to two hours just to have German goons rushing up and down the ranks trying to arrive at the same count and getting a different one each time.

We soon tired of the game of moving one person up in the ranks ahead of the counting guard and then popping up to be counted twice so that the poor fellow got one too many or one too few, if we did it in reverse. This was amusing in the fine weather but, as the days grew colder, we just wanted to get back inside the fort as soon as possible.

Finally, when it was winter and bitterly cold, we had a Red Cross blanket each and used to take it with us on parade to keep from freezing in the sub-zero temperatures.

We were issued with one Kommisarbrot between five per day, and there was always some discussion about cutting the loaf up so that everyone got an equal share and the outside shares would be rotated so that each person had a turn of the two outside ends.

There were times when someone would miss out because often the share was one loaf between six, or maybe one loaf between four, according to the available supplies sent to the fort from the baker.

We also had a mess-tin of swede soup, with masses of diced swedes, cut into half inch squares, cooked in water. Sometimes potatoes were diced in with the swedes but mostly not. The mess-tin of water usually contained about twenty squares of swede, not very much to live on.

Once a week we had a meat soup, which was the swede soup to which had been added a very small quantity of meat, usually horse meat, so that one was lucky indeed to find an actual lump of meat, usually triumphantly held up in the spoon by the owner. Because the soup contained a fair number of small cockroaches, it could happen that the slivers of meat would be thrown out with them; we were never so hungry that we would eat the cockroaches on purpose, but never so full that we left any edible part of the soup.

The cookhouse was fairly swarming with cockroaches,

because this was the only regularly warm place in the fort, there being no means of heating such a huge building, and a quantity of the cockroaches always seemed to find their way into the huge cauldron that cooked our soup and they in turn were cooked and served up with the soup.

We also had pretty well as much coffee as we wanted; this sounds better than it was because the coffee was ersatz acorn variety which had no relation to the type we know and love, and which, if allowed to get too cool, would develop into a disgusting brown slimy sludge which was totally undrinkable.

We had butter and honey to spread on our bread. This, too, sounds better than it was, because the honey and the butter were entirely artificial, bearing only a superficial resemblance in taste and texture to the real thing.

Both the honey and the butter were a triumph of German ingenuity and, as such, had to be admired.

By November 1940 the rigours of the past six months had taken their toll on me and I had to take stock of my situation.

In May 1940 I had been about thirteen stone in weight, just over six foot tall, with very little fat and a large amount of muscle; by now I estimated that my weight was down to about eleven stone and I was losing a lot of strength.

I desperately needed more food and exercise.

On the plus side, I was listening to the guards as much as possible and my German was better than it had ever been, even though I had to practice it under my breath, and I was able to distinguish regional accents and, if necessary, mimic them.

I could speak the type of German that the peasants and the soldiers spoke, with the same colloquial shortcuts that we use in English without thinking, and in all languages, such things as 'can't' instead of 'cannot'. 'Wie geht es ihnen' became 'wie gehts', for 'how are you'. 'Einmal' became 'mal', for 'once', and so on.

I had always had the facility of absorbing and reproducing speech, sometimes unconsciously, so that I adopted an accent without thinking about it. In the past, in the army, this had often annoyed my friends, who used to think that I was teasing them. A Glaswegian, whose accent I had unconsciously mimicked, came up to me once and thrust his face close to mine and said, very belligerently, 'Are youse taking the mickey?'. I had to reassure him that no, I was not taking the mickey, I simply admired his Scottish accent, which was quite untrue.

The Scot is the most sensitive, I think, of almost anyone else in the world when it comes to fierce national pride, and he is often on the offensive when he need not be. This appears to be exaggerated in the army, where Sassenachs are openly despised and anyone who is unfortunate enough not to be a Scot is looked down on as an alien.

If I were to be talking with a couple of Geordies, for example, from Northumberland, I would very quickly lapse into their distinctive accent without being conscious of doing so.

Attitudes when speaking are also important, Frenchmen use certain gestures and hold their lips in certain ways when speaking, move their hands in a very distinctive fashion when emphasizing a point.

The Italians use different hand gestures and expressions.

Germans have a distinctive way of holding their heads when making a point and of nodding and shaking a forefinger in warning, with the palm of the hand towards them; the English shake a finger with the palm at right angles, and the Italians often, but not always, have the palms turned downward or away from them.

It is the little things that characterize a nation or an ethnic group, and if one is to merge into that group, it is necessary to mimic their idiosyncrasies.

I was also learning some Polish, enough to make myself understood.

I had been taught a recognition song in Polish, but, of necessity, I had to learn it purely phonetically.

It was here that my schooling helped, because the eight lines of poetry or text we had to learn every single day on pain of a beating had trained my memory so that learning a few lines of a song was easy, and, to this day, I can still remember the song, together with all the myriad of verse and prose that was crammed into my mind at school.

The Polish song was a means to make contact with the Polish underground and was not widely known as such, so it was safe to use for some time.

I had great confidence in my German. Before the war I had only a smattering and very little interest in learning more, but after I joined the army I really got down to learning speech essentials, as opposed to writing, and on my course was able to practice with a German prisoner of war in England until I became really expert, understanding the language enough to think wholly in German and to swear, using a German word, if I accidentally tripped.

I was able to develop a rough sort of East Prussian accent which would have made any German language teacher weep, but which was spoken by the labourers and soldiery and the farm peasants to the extent that it was impossible to classify me as coming from any region or having any single dialect, but, at the same time, I would probably be accepted at face value by the people beside whom I intended to work.

Chapter 4

1941

One thing I had learnt about the German character was the implicit trust that Germans place in documents and authority.

If one is definite and has some sort of documentary evidence to wave around, then a forceful assertion is going to be believed regardless. I think that this attitude of the German is partly an inbred respect and fear of authority and a result of the fear and hierarchical domination encouraged by the Nazi Party with the rise of the National Socialist ideas.

A German in authority will expect immediate obedience without question and will usually get it, just as he will obey implicitly any order from a higher authority; this is a part of the German character which can be exploited and from an apparent strength it can become a weakness.

We were getting roll calls only twice a day now, but they were still taking at least an hour and at regular intervals we would be subjected to a pep talk by the German Kommandant, Oberst (Colonel) Mackensen, who was a short and rather pompous officer who had a very good command of the English language, who studied the expressions and idioms of the prisoners with great interest and who liked to hear the sound of his own voice speaking English to the prisoners.

Consequently he would go on for a very long time about all sorts of subjects, listened to with admiration by his junior officers, but usually with extreme impatience and boredom by the prisoners.

There is a story about this man which has probably been retold with delight by many POWs.

The incident occurred when a party of German soldiers were ordered to rip up the floor of one of the rooms to look for hidden tools which had been missing from the carpenter's shop. I don't think they found anything but at the end of the exercise, after all the prisoners were back in their rooms, they discovered that a hammer was missing from their tools.

The Kommandant had the whole camp assembled and vowed that they would stand out in the cold for as long as it took to find the missing hammer. Eventually after some hours the hammer was found and after a further interval the guards were paraded in force in the compound; so, too, were all the German officers. The Kommandant arrived last and strutted up on to his rostrum and held the hammer, now polished and burnished to new condition, high in the air for all to see.

"Vell, chentlemen," he said, "as you see ve haf found ze hammer. Our Cherman intelligence iss better zan you sink. To use your own idiom, you sink zat ve know fock nossing, vell you are wrong, ve know fock all . . ."

One can hardly expect the Germans to understand the contradictory English language which would be the most illogical in the world. This was further stressed by a British soldier who was forced to broadcast by the Germans and whose speech was rigidly censored with dire threats if he departed from the script by a single word, but he still sent the message along these lines: '. . . . and the German Army cannot fail to conquer the Allies. Tell that to the Army, to the Navy, to the Air Force, and, above all, tell it to the Marines.'

My name had been down for a working party in the town or the surrounding area, and I did eventually get on to a working party digging trenches for drains. This sounds pretty mundane but it was exactly what I wanted because it allowed me to exercise, to get more food, to look at the surrounding landscape and above all to try to make some contact with the Polish Underground.

We were closely guarded by the more able-bodied of the guards and our squad of fifteen men had four guards, an Obergefreiter (corporal), a Gefreiter (lance-corporal) and two Schutzer (privates). One of the privates was a Westphalian farmer who would have been about twenty-one and was stockily built and very keen on Arbeit, the German word for work, which is a minor deity in Germany where work for work's sake is the rule. He had a horrific wound in the neck where a bullet had passed from just below his jaw out through his cheek, affecting his speech and eating habits, but he looked as strong as an ox.

We were split up into pairs and an area was measured off so that we had each to dig a cubic metre in two hours. There was a small railway by the side of us containing rows of skips, each holding two cubic metres, and the idea was that the two of us had to fill up each skip in the two-hour period.

This was reasonable because the soil was very sandy and easy to dig. On the other hand, we were not used to the exercise and were considerably weaker than we had thought.

The bloke with me was a rather weedy individual who had been a clerk in an office in London and he was obviously feeling the task was too much for him.

I could see that the Westphalian guard was watching him closely and I was expecting that the guard would threaten him for getting behind all the others. However, what happened was quite unexpected.

The guard unslung his rifle from his shoulder, put his head and one arm through the sling and had the rifle slung across his back. He then told the clerk to get out of the trench and he himself got down to shovelling the sand into the skip with such vigour and evident enjoyment that we all stopped work and watched. I believe that he would have done this for all of us just for the joy of working!

A cubic metre of sandy earth weighs about a ton, so that we had to move a ton of earth every two hours from about eight am to four pm, eight hours, and we had a break about every two hours, but the food we had was much better, supplied by the contractor; although at first it was a chore and we came back to camp each night with blistered hands and aching backs, after about two or three weeks we enjoyed it and found that we could handle that amount of work quite easily.

I regained most of my weight and increased my strength and endurance and put my name down for a transport.

This meant that I wanted to be shipped to some more distant location, ideally a farm where I would have a lot better chance of getting some contacts with the Poles.

I had chosen my time badly because it was now January 1941, mid-winter, with the bitter winds sweeping across from the Russian plains and freezing everything solid.

My first transport turned out to be a logging camp in the middle of a large forest of pines where we were engaged in felling, trimming and loading the logs for transport to the railway lines about two miles away.

The timber was cut with large crosscut saws operated by one of us at each end, pulling alternately until the tree was almost cut through and then hammering in wedges until the tree fell; then we would trim off all the branches with axes, saw the trunks into twelve-foot lengths and load them onto a timber wagon, or sometimes just hitch a chain round three or four of them and get the horse to drag them to a clearing for loading later.

There were about a hundred Poles working on this job and I was very well situated to make some contact. All I had to do was to convince the Polish underground that I was not a German 'plant' and that I was able to cooperate with their activities and, when they were needing supplies, I could give them the necessary information to radio for a drop at a pre-arranged site.

I went about it very cautiously and got to know quite a number of the Poles, to get the feel of their attitudes.

When I had decided that a particular Pole might be the one I was after, I casually whistled the tune of the song I had been taught, and waited to get the necessary response.

What happened in fact was quite remarkable.

A young Pole of about fifteen with a foot deformity appeared to seek my company more than one would expect in the normal course of working, and one day he said that he had an elder brother who worked nearby and would I like to meet him, because he could get some schnapps and wurst, the two items of which were the sum total of bliss to most of the Poles and Germans alike.

I should mention that the schnapps was something that sensible people avoided as much as possible because it was distilled illicitly from potatoes and had a very high alcohol content with mind-boggling results.

The German idea of this was summed up in the popular phrase 'mit einem Liter Schnaps und einem Stückchen Wurst hat man die ganze Welt': with a litre of schnapps and a piece of sausage one has all one needs in the world.

I agreed that I would like to meet his brother and went along with him, telling the guard that I was going to the railhead to work, which we did occasionally and with only the one guard we had a lot of freedom of movement; but if we did escape there was nowhere to go in that forest. In mid-winter we would have lasted three or four days at the most before freezing to death.

The brother was about twenty years old and looked fit enough to have been taken into the army, but at that time there were quite a few able-bodied Poles around, mostly in reserve occupations or with specialized knowledge which kept them out of the armed forces.

We chatted in German, which most Poles seemed to have as a second language in this area, and it was not long before I got the opportunity to whistle my tune, just casually and in a preoccupied way.

"That's a Polish tune," he said, "do you know the words?"

I accordingly sang the first verse which I give here in phonetic spelling, which was the way I learnt it:

'Gdy vrooteesh, por teelo glugich lata,'
'Sashtanish porqui vkeearta,'
'Yak gdibi nigedi neets.'

I waited breathlessly to see whether he complied with the next part of the recognition song and he sang:

'Gdy vrooteesh, o neece me neer zapeetash,'
'Poproshdu meer pchveetash,'
'Yak gdibi nigedi neets.'

The text in Polish of these two verses goes as follows:

'Gdy wrocisz'
'Po tylu dlugich latach'
'Zastaniesz pokoj w kwiatach'
'Jak gdyby nigdy nic.'

'Gdy wrocisz'
'O nic mnie nie zapytach'
'Po prostu mnie przywitasz'
'Jak gdyby nigdy nic.'

The translation into English is as follows:

When you come back
After many long years
You will find a room full of flowers
As if nothing had changed.

When you come back
I will ask you nothing
We will simply say hallo
As if nothing had changed.

We shook hands and he said he wanted me to meet his boss in a couple of days and I went back to the work feeling very wobbly in my stomach but elated that I had at long last made contact.

The uncertainties were enormous. Suppose that this was a plant from the Gestapo and the Polish underground had been busted? Maybe this was the way the Germans were

49

sorting out any possible saboteurs or agents or any subversive elements? These and hundreds of other possibilities were buzzing through my brain as I mechanically carried on with my work back at the camp site.

Two days went by and nothing happened. Then three more days and I asked the youngster what was going on with his brother but all he would say was *'powoli, powoli'*, with the accent very much on the long second syllable; in Polish this means 'slowly, slowly', a very popular word with the Poles at this time, particularly if I was working with them and going too fast at the job, they would tell me to slow down.

Finally after a week I was told to go and see the brother, and once more I signalled to the guard that I was going to the rail-head.

The guard was a rather miserable type who obviously had problems with the cold weather. He had a thick scarf wrapped round his neck and his field service cap was unfolded so as to fit over his ears and button under his chin. He also wore thick woollen gloves and would frequently raise his hands to cover his nose and mouth and would blow warm air into them. In spite of all this, his nose dripped continuously and all he could do to keep warm was to stamp around in the wood chips muttering derogatory expletives about Poland, the weather and the war.

When I called to him and pointed to the rail-head he just jerked his head and I went off out of sight.

I met the brother and after we had chatted for a bit a very burly character appeared and lumbered over to us and shook hands but he did not say who he was, not even a Christian name.

He spoke reasonable English and we chatted for some time about England, where I lived, what my father did, where I went to school, what my regiment was, battalion, company, platoon, section leader, army number and a whole lot of other details which I forget now but at the time I was speaking to him it all seemed to flow like a normal conversation and, even though I realized that I was being interrogated, it was all very light-veined and even jocular.

Back at the camp that evening I thought of my parents.

For all I knew they had not heard any news about me.

There was no guarantee that the German Red Cross had sent back my details, or that any of the many letters I had written had ever arrived at home. We had none of the much talked about Red Cross Parcels and certainly no letters or communication from home. If the German guards were to be believed, then England could already be in the hands of the Germans.

I thought to hell with it all. I was going ahead with whatever happened; my future was extremely uncertain anyway and I had little hope of surviving this war, so I was going to do all I could to make things difficult for everyone . . . etc. etc. I wrote back home that all was well and that I was fit and that I was being well-treated by the Germans and that I hoped to be home soon and not to worry about me and so on.

In fact, it had been reported to my parents that I was missing, believed killed in action, and it was not until almost a year later that they received news that I had been registered as a British prisoner of war and they got some of my letters after that.

At this time I was a bit depressed, especially as I had been having dreams about home and waking up from a nightmare thinking that the whole business had been a bad dream and that I was back home in England . . . and then finding that I was in Poland and that the dream was a reality. I was only twenty years old and was finding it hard to take at this time; if only I had known what lay ahead I would probably have chickened out but I developed a sort of philosophy that I would live each day as it came along and ignore any thoughts of the future or any hopes of survival after the war. I honestly believe that this philosophy helped my survival; by knowing that I could not survive made the present always better than the future and therefore bearable.

Two days later and back at work with the cold and miserable guard still wiping his dripping nose, I once again signalled to him that I was going to the railhead and he waved agreement, so I strolled off, met the brother, who was waiting for me, and we just kept walking deeper and deeper into the forest.

We must have walked for two hours, fairly briskly, and possibly covered about ten miles when we came to a small wooden hut in a clearing. It was here that I met Jan Tarasov, a Pole with a Russian surname, who was a metal engineer, ex-captain in the Polish army, about five foot eleven, well-built, mousy hair and fresh pink complexion. We were to work together and to rely on each other absolutely.

We laid low in the hut for some days and, on bicycles, made our way out of the forest to a farmhouse on the edge of the tree line. I had absolutely no idea where I was.

In the farmhouse I changed into civilian clothes: a cloth cap with a large peak bent into an inverted V, a fairly coarse but warm flannel shirt, cotton long johns, cotton undersocks and woollen oversocks, wide almost bell-bottomed trousers with bicycle clips of a kind that I had not seen before which held the trousers tight round the ankle but left a fold sticking out at right angles on each side of the leg. I had a pair of rather flash black leather boots with steel caps, worn by factory workers, a thin woollen pullover with no sleeves and a thin baggy jacket sort of greyish colour. Over this I wore a navy blue thick type of duffel coat but fastened with large buttons instead of toggles.

My papers consisted of merely a work permit in the name of Jan Zblevsky, born in Marienberg in East Prussia, aged 23 years, suffering from pulmonary tuberculosis, a carpenter by trade but doing odd repair work. This was a common enough occupation and anyway anyone was doing any job he could get, preferably indoors out of the cold. I had a bicycle with high handlebars and a brief case, old, greasy and battered, in which I kept a bottle of cold tea and a packet of sandwiches and which fastened on to the bike with the flap over the crossbar to dangle between my knees. It was the first time that I had seen this arrangement and I was quite impressed. I also had about forty German Reichmark and some small change in pfennig.

We had a job to do in Grudziadz, which the Germans had sensibly renamed Graudenz. The place of work was a metal foundry and factory for cables and heavy machinery called Firma Vensky.

When we arrived in Graudenz we went to a sort of barracks where the workers were billeted six to a room, but at least we each had a bed and a couple of blankets and all our meals were obtained at the works canteen, but we could buy bread and sausage at the shops in the town which, however, I never visited, because they were owned by Poles and they would have spotted me for something out of the ordinary and probably have reported me for their own safety. It was not unusual for the Germans to pose as escaped prisoners of war and then punish anyone of the Poles who had helped them hide away.

Chapter 5

1941

My first day started at 7.30 in the morning, still dark and very cold, lining up at the entrance to Firma Vensky, to be checked by the German guards.

It was the first time I had ever used forged papers, and I couldn't tell whether I was shaking from the cold or from anxiety, but I need not have worried because the glance from the German guard was very superficial and Jan was chatting away to me in Polish and I was nodding and grinning as we showed our papers.

The German authorities had decreed that only German was to be spoken by the work force and they generally frowned upon anyone speaking Polish; but it was a stupid rule because a number of Poles couldn't speak German and wouldn't learn, so most of the guards just ignored the rule.

In this case the guard couldn't have cared less about anything; all he wanted to do was to check everyone as quickly as possible and then get back to the warm guardhouse.

We went through very quickly and then we were inside the factory grounds.

The early weeks were spent in a variety of jobs and really

just gave me some idea of the routine and the layout of the factory, which was huge and must have produced most of the heavy-metal products in Poland.

There was everything from prefabricated bridge sections to roof girders, and every type of extruded wire for cables, huge masses of pig-iron piled up in every available corner of the yards, together with rods, angles, flats and anything else you like to name except that there was no military hardware in the form of weapons or tank parts, although all types of agricultural machinery were there.

Because of the warmth, the smelting areas were very popular work places and these were the areas in which I was most interested. The moulds were always lined with a grey or black graphite powder so that the solidified product was able to slip out of the mould easily and the next pouring could then be done without any chipping or breaking of the mould casing.

Preparation of the mould was usually given to non-skilled workers although the product could be rendered useless if the graphite was too thick or uneven. It was necessary to pass an air hose over the mould before use to blow away any excess graphite, but if the air hose were to be held too close to the casing at any stage the graphite would all be blown away at that point and it was probable that the casing would have to be broken to extract the casting.

Jan and I got onto this job and we worked very hard at it and became so efficient that the skilled foundrymen wanted us to prepare the moulds for them rather than any casuals, and they relied on us to have the moulds prepared so that they could just do the pouring and thus increase their output and not waste time on checking and air-blasting the mould casings.

When there was a suitable batch of castings, as, for example, agricultural implements, we would mix some grease with the graphite powder and put it in the mould so that the metal castings would surround the lump of graphite and this would present an implement that was going to fracture very soon after use and was virtually untraceable prior to fracture.

We were doing about two hundred castings a day, so the quantity of useless goods was about twenty five per cent of the daily product and was stored outside for about a month and then shipped by train to places all over the country, where they would be distributed to the farmers or engineers or builders.

We did bridge, ship, train and carriage parts, barrack roof prefab struts, and a hundred and one other types of moulded metal castings and we were such keen workers that we were eventually put on to the cable section, which was the main part of the factory.

We had to work a machine that wound insulating material on to the wires and it was not long before we were producing some of the most unreliable cables in the country.

In typical German fashion the cable was tested regularly, using a type of 'post office box' which measured resistance and conductivity. In fact so regularly that we were told when the next test was going to be done so that we could have the drum ready and waste no time. The test drums of cable were always superb and passed the tests with flying colours.

It never occurred to the Germans to test a random sample, thank goodness, and by the time they got round to using the dud stuff we hoped we would be long gone.

Our sojourn at Graudenz was a very busy one and I had gained a lot of confidence and the weather was improving so we volunteered to work outside on the cable gangs, which was much harder work but provided better opportunities to get out and about the countryside. It was certainly unwise to stay in one work situation for too long.

For this particular job we travelled back towards Torun to a fairly isolated area on the banks of the river Vistula, which is one of the fastest flowing rivers in the world, full of eddies and currents.

The purpose of the job was to supply power to a military barracks and installations on the far side of the river, where there was no source of electricity readily available.

This involved digging trenches, filling up skips with the dirt and carting it away by train. Then rigging up the underwater cable, which was a highly specialized type of cable (manufactured by Firma Vensky of course) consisting of six high power electric cables, suitably insulated, measuring in all about three inches in diameter, and cased with a waterproofed material which was like a tube of oilskin, but much thicker, into which was pumped a continuous supply of oil so that the underlying cabling could not be contaminated by the water.

This necessitated a small pumping station, which was securely fenced off, containing a thousand gallon oil tank, and a pump which operated on a pressure valve so that the oil in the cable case was always at the correct pressure.

Since oil was a very valuable commodity the whole area was supervised by four SS guards, wearing the *'Totenkopf'*, a representation of a skull in silver metal, as a badge on the front of their peaked service caps and with SS lightning flashes on their lapels. They were a very suspicious lot, poking into everything and seeming to be everywhere at once.

The cable had to be pulled across the Vistula and, since it was a distance of about three hundred yards from shore to shore, a light line was brought across from the other side and securely bolted to the cable end, then pulled by a donkey engine on the far bank. The cable had cork floats attached to it every ten yards or so to ensure that it would not drag on the river bed while being pulled across; the floats would then be removed when the cable spanned the river and the weight of the cable would ensure that it rested securely on the river bottom.

I had volunteered to stand thigh deep in the water and from there a line of Poles stretched back to the cable drum and we all had to guide and pull the cable to take some of the strain off the donkey engine.

I had a short-blade knife and was able to make a series of cuts through the casing while it was out of sight under the water so that, when the job was complete, the pump would be sending an enormous amount of the precious oil into the now faulty casing and thence into the river itself. The speed of the current would not allow the oil to surface for some miles downstream.

I was told later that the power supply to the military installations over there was never very reliable and subject to failures which were attributed to leaks in the casing or to inadequate oil supply. But it was certain that the quantity of oil needed for that project would have been prohibitive. They must have required enormous quantities of electricity to make it necessary to have a mains supply rather than individual generators.

In fact, in six months, someone had put a hole in the tank, the oil had drained away, water had got into the cable and effectively rendered it useless. Six Poles were subsequently shot for sabotage, but it was only a gesture on the part of the Germans, because the Poles were probably innocent, and the SS guards would have been sent on active duty to the front as their punishment had they not found a scapegoat.

During this time the Polish underground were receiving quantities of weapons and explosives, including some of the new plastic explosive, which was very popular because one could treat it like putty, which it resembled, except that it had a smell reminiscent of marzipan, and it was so safe that it could be carried in one's pocket, thrown around, moulded into any shape and generally treated like a bit of trash; however, a surprisingly small bit of it could cause quite a disproportionately large explosion.

The detonators were quite another story, and had to be treated with the greatest care. They were pushed into the plastic and their ends were pinched in to start the fuse, which was variable in time from a risky five minutes to as long as an hour.

We had some special fuses which were constructed to go over the surface of a railway line. Thus we could mould a length of plastic explosive on either side of the rail, pretty well out of sight, and push an instantaneous fuse over the rail face and into each side moulding of plastic, so that when a train went over the fuse the explosive detonated almost immediately, usually just under the driver's platform; the force of the plastic was sufficient to lift the rear of the engine off the rails, to buckle the rail itself and consequently to derail the whole train.

Power houses were the prime targets but anything that could disrupt the workings of the Third Reich was fair game.

Things were getting a bit dangerous for Jan and me by this time and we decided that we would split up and take a holiday. By this we meant that we would get jobs that were fairly innocuous and not subject to any great security risks.

Accordingly I got a job on a building site in the suburbs of Graudenz, and for a while I was a brickie's labourer and later a brickie, although a very poor one. I dug a lot of trenches, filled a lot of skips, and at one time had the enviable job of driving a little diesel train which pulled the skips.

I can remember that to start the train one had to switch on the diesel fuel, then unscrew a sort of tap in the engine block which came right out. I would then roll up a small square of pink blotting paper which had been treated with saltpetre, touch it with the lighted end of my cigarette till it fizzed, then screw it back into the socket of the train engine and swing a starting handle which turned the flywheel and the train engine would start.

It was really most enjoyable to have that job as an engine driver. I suppose it satisfied a boyhood dream or something like that.

The engine was quite small, about six foot long and a bit over a yard wide, with a little cabin for the driver, with a seat and levers in front of the seat consisting of a throttle, a brake and a reverse and forward lever coupled to the throttle so that it was impossible to put it into reverse at full throttle. All in all it was made to be driven sedately with the simplest possible controls. Much to my delight it also had a whistle to warn the workers when it started to move off or if someone was on the rail ahead.

My job was to go to the engine first thing each morning,

take off the canvas covering and place it, carefully folded up in the best traditions of Deutsches Ordnung (German orderliness), in one corner of the little 'engineer's shed'.

I was the 'engineer' — anyone driving a train in Germany was graced with that title. I would then take off my jacket, fold it carefully and hide it at the back of the shed so that the casual passer-by could not knock it off. I would then get a large oilcan and oil every possible part of the engine and wipe carefully so that no wasteful trickles of oil showed. This and precautions similar to this were necessary because any German, be he Gestapo, Party Member, Overseer, Hitler Jugend (especially the Hitler Youth) or just plain nosey parker might take it upon himself to report anything that looked like wastefulness or dereliction of duty.

Next I had to get a grease gun and grease all the skip wheels and tipping mechanism. I would then put the skips in the upright position; they had been left overnight tipped at right angles in case it rained.

Then I would start up the engine and drive slowly to the work area where the rails had been shifted at the end of the previous day's work to the new area for excavation.

Each worker had two metres square by one metre deep to dig out and load into the skip which would only hold one cubic metre weighing just one ton.

I did not get away with just watching them load, I had to dig and load just one cubic metre and then take the train to the unloading point which was about a hundred yards up the line, over a raised ramp where trucks could come close in to the lines. I could then unlatch each skip and, with the help of the truck driver, tip the contents of the skip straight into the back of the truck. Having unloaded two skips in this way, the truck driver would move the truck forward for the next two skips and so on until the truck was full when it would drive off and be replaced by an empty truck.

During all this time the diggers would be having a rest and a smoke until I brought the train back to the work site for the next load.

The number of skips varied but it was not unusual to have about twenty at a time, and I imagine that the little diesel engine could easily pull double this number on the level.

Sometimes we had the truck loading area downhill from the work site, and it became quite difficult to control the train to prevent it from accelerating under the weight of more than twenty tons behind the engine.

If such a situation developed it was my responsibility to get one of the gang to ride the last skip with a piece of timber stuck in the wheels to act as a brake.

It was during just such a situation that I drove too fast round a slight bend and derailed together with about twenty fully loaded skips.

The result was fairly spectacular and, had I not jumped from the engine to the left, as it was falling over to the right, I would have ended up under the engine or under the fully laden skips which piled up on to the back of the little diesel engine.

The German boss was absolutely livid with rage and swore that I had deliberately crashed the train. He grabbed me and sent someone for the police.

Before I knew it I was in the local police station and the German who had employed me on the building site was calling me a saboteur and threatening me with the Gestapo.

I had left my papers behind in my jacket with my money and I felt that this was no time to say where they were or try to prove my innocence, because this German was very angry indeed and was after my blood.

He kept me in the police station for three hours and then a car arrived and two civilians got out and came into the room.

One of them, a short stocky little fellow with a Hitler moustache, wasted no time but came over to me and thrust his face up to mine asking for papers. When I shook my head he belted me across the face and stopped me from falling by grabbing my shirt, tearing it down the front and exposing my prisoner of war disc and my army identity discs on a shoelace round my neck.

He stared at me for a few moments, then, without another word, he bundled me out of the police station into his car and, accompanied by his silent companion, we drove off.

Shortly we reached the town and I was led up some steps and into a room with a desk and a few chairs.

There was a German soldier with SS badges and a rifle who stood at my side, and the two civilians, who were clearly Gestapo, started to interrogate me in German.

I said, in atrocious German, that I was a British prisoner of war, and that I did not understand much German, that I had escaped from a working party, and that I had been living roughly, keeping out of sight of everyone and hoping to jump a train to take me to France.

I had to admit to myself that this was not a very convincing story but I was not prepared for the sudden explosion that happened in my mouth and for the abrupt way in which I found myself lying on the floor.

However, when I saw the butt of the guard's rifle about six inches from my face, I realized that he had hit me with it in the mouth, knocking out my two front teeth and splitting the inside of my upper lip so that my mouth was soon filled with blood.

I suppose I must have just lain there looking at the guard in a daze, because the civilian shouldered him aside and grabbed my shirt again pulling me back into the chair.

"You are a saboteur and you have damaged some German property. You will tell me to whom you report and where you come from." The Gestapo said this in English in a quiet voice. Lucky for me, I thought, at least he has accepted that I am English.

I said that I had been captured at Calais and had escaped from a working party and that my photograph and fingerprints had been taken by the Wehrmacht and that I had a prisoner of war number 8136, and I showed him the disc.

This time I was on the floor with a rapidly swelling left temple from a blow by the civilian.

And so the interrogation went on with me replying in

English most of the time, and with them asking the questions in German and pretending they didn't understand me, whilst I was pretending I didn't understand them.

After what seemed like ages but was probably only half an hour or so, the guard was told to take me to the lock-up.

We went down to the basement with the guard prodding me hard in the back every few steps and I was locked in an empty room with absolutely nothing in it and with drab coloured walls that had at some time long ago had some sort of wallpaper with an unrecognizable faded pattern.

There was a small window high up but too narrow to climb out of — even if I had the energy to jump up to it.

It is a strange thing that in times of great stress one tends to notice trivial little details with great clarity.

I can remember at my prep school, when I was waiting to have a caning, I noticed a butterfly which was trapped in the window of the headmaster's study, and that butterfly was visible in great detail and colour, almost enhanced as if under a searchlight; it was the same with that wallpaper and it became important to me to try to see some sort of pattern on the wall.

I was expecting to be taken out and shot because, in spite of my story, I was in civilian clothing, which I must have got from somewhere, and my story of stealing it from a house in the country and not remembering or knowing where, was about as unbelievable as it could be. There was also the question of my papers; they had been quite well made and, should they be found and brought in, any story of finding them in the jacket pocket would certainly not be believed.

I hoped that the money with the papers would be sufficient for whoever found the jacket to hang on to it and not turn it over to the authorities. I think this must have been the case because I was not confronted with the jacket or any papers.

I was not surprised but I was very apprehensive when the guard came to fetch me, with a rather wolfish grin on his face, and marched me out into the street and along the roadway for about half a mile to a large barracks.

I asked him where we were going and his smile broadened as he pointed his rifle at me and went through the motion of shooting.

I honestly believed at that moment that I was being taken to a place for execution.

1938 — New recruit (extreme right).

1939.

1943 — On Staub's farm.

1944 — Stalag XXa (seated with legs crossed).

1944 — Neweheimat.

Chapter 6

1941

I was taken into an office and handed over to a Feldwebel who motioned me to sit on a bench after putting the contents of my trouser pockets on a desk top. There was nothing incriminating in my pockets, and anyway I had no option, so I did as requested and the Feldwebel signed a paper and my guard walked out.

After an hour or so, during which several soldiers came and went, looking at me curiously as I sat on the bench, very miserable and sorry for myself with a very much bashed-up face and a big thick lip, the Feldwebel answered a phone on his desk and then motioned me to follow him into a room.

When I got in I found that there was a Hauptmann (captain) sitting behind his desk busily writing.

We both stood stiffly to attention until he looked up, studied my face with a deadpan expression for a few moments, then nodded to the Feldwebel to go.

He did a bit more writing and then looked up and said, in good English, "You are a very lucky young man. The Gestapo have checked your story and confirmed that you are an English prisoner of war. I have a copy of your photograph here and the record of your number which tallies with the disc you have there. You are lucky that the Gestapo have turned you over to us; they would have been quite justified in having you shot as a spy. You will be returned to your Stalag for punishment."

The Feldwebel collected me and I was taken to their canteen and given some potato soup with meat in it which I would have enjoyed except that my mouth was so sore that each mouthful had to be gulped down to avoid the pain.

It was interesting that the Wehrmacht soldiers were quite sympathetic towards me and I heard several of them mention the Gestapo with some distaste and shaking of heads. It emphasized to me the feeling that there was no love lost between the military and the secret police.

A guard was then detailed to take me to the lock-up in the barracks. These lock-ups were usually basement cells in which vegetables had been stored in the past, because they still retained the smell of old bad cabbage and potatoes, and they had very little in the way of ventilation so the smell persisted, coupled with the smell of the latrine bucket in one corner.

The officer had evidently phoned through to Fort 17 Kommandantura because the next day one of the Stalag guards came along to pick me up and we had a train journey to go back to Torun.

During the journey the poor guard got a few suspicious looks from the civilians who saw my face and evidently thought that he had been beating me up, but they were too afraid to say or do anything other than to give me a blink of sympathy when the guard was not looking.

The blink of sympathy is universally used in Poland and Germany, and probably in other parts of Europe, and consists of looking at a person and then blinking both eyes together, accompanied by a slight nod and a kindly look, sometimes a conspiratorial look.

In this case, it was followed by a glare at the guard, or a stony stare or a whisper to a companion.

Finally we arrived at Torun station and walked to a different Fort, 13, which was very similar to 17 in structure. Apparently the old place had been cleared out and I made a mental note to find out why. We went in through the large entrance gate and straight up to the Kommandantura office where I was left waiting on a wooden form outside the Kommandant's room.

I waited about an hour during which time I noticed how much bustling activity went on in and around this office.

German army clerks were hurrying back and forth around the various offices and each one always seemed to have the same sheaf of papers in his left hand. Presumably this was in order to leave his other hand free for saluting. When an officer came by they would stand back against the wall of the passage and salute smartly. At the same time they would click their heels by rising up on their toes, pivoting their heels outwards and then bringing them together with a sharp click and timing their salute so that the fingers touched the forehead at the same time that the heels clicked together.

I had to get up each time an officer came by and stand to attention, and they would look at me closely, knowing that I was not a civilian in spite of my clothes, but knowing also that, in the British Army, no one saluted without a hat on.

Eventually I was told to enter the Kommandant's office and I stood rigidly to attention in front of his desk.

He delivered a homily on the foolishness of trying to escape and reiterated that I was lucky not to be punished by the Gestapo and he sentenced me to two weeks in the bunker.

So I was taken down to the punishment cells with the old familiar smell of rotting potatoes and cabbages, and I was given a new uniform consisting of British Army trousers, shirt, socks, boots, battledress top and forage cap; all of them far from new but obviously straight out of the delouser, with the typical scorched smell, and I was also given a package tied up with string, containing my private 'effects'; a pencil, my 'AB 64', which was my army pay book, containing a list of my inoculations and pay prior to entering active service, all with the unit names carefully blacked out; I really don't know why I kept it. Also there were a number of letters, the first ever from home, which I had not known about, and which made me very happy because I realized that my parents now knew that I was safe in a POW camp and not killed in action.

My mother had written all the news of home, being careful not to include anything that might have been considered military information, such as where my brother David was, or what the war news was, or anything like that.

But she did convey to me that the back garden of the house in Hampstead was now used to grow vegetables and that various relatives had asked after me, and that my school, a Catholic Grammar School, had a special Mass said for my welfare, and daily read out the news to the assembled school, with special reference to old boys now in the Army, Navy and Air Force.

I recall that I was very much upset by the reminder of my home life and the expectation that I would never see it again, so much so that the guard occasionally found me in tears and thought that the punishment was the cause, saying things like 'Oh, *Junge, Junge, Junge*, you should learn to take your punishment like a man.' This cheered me up quite a bit to think that I minded being alone when in fact I quite enjoyed the chance of being uninterrupted in my train of thought and I was able to see out the two weeks quite happily.

When finally I emerged from the bunker, it was almost like leaving a secure little haven and getting out into the great wide world of the camp activity.

Red Cross parcels had been arriving and, although it was known that the German authorities helped themselves to quite a lot of the parcels, yet there were enough to allow one parcel between two men.

As a reward for attempting to escape, and also because I had missed so many of the issues, the British camp commandant allowed me to have a whole parcel to myself.

These parcels were about fifteen inches by seven inches by seven inches deep and packed with goodies which we had only dreamed about, like tea, milk powder, sugar, tinned butter, chocolate, cheese, fish paste, meat loaf, sardines, cocoa, salt, pepper, and coffee, real live one hundred per cent coffee, which was worth its weight in gold to barter with the guards for bread. At one time a small tin of coffee would buy six loaves, which the guard supplied one at a time each day for six days, being very careful that he was not caught because there was a severe penalty for bartering with the prisoners.

There was also an indication of the sort of thing that England must be getting used to, as a wartime measure, the issue of powdered eggs, which was apparently dehydrated yolk that could be reconstituted by adding water but tasted very unlike the real product. However, it was all wonderful to us at the time and provided a much needed link with home.

We also had issues of cigarettes in tins of fifty.

It seemed that life for all these living skeletons was going to improve so much that they would get fat and lazy and want to stay guests of the German Reich forever.

It was amazing how the topic of conversation shifted from food to other things once the Red Cross parcels were established in their delivery to the prisoners.

There were now theatre groups and language groups, choirs and woodworking groups, and pretty soon the morale was really quite good.

The watery potato soup could now be supplemented by some of the contents of the Red Cross parcels and made to taste palatable and even nutritious, and there were cookhouse issues of tea already milked and sugared as in the army.

Thank God for the Red Cross!

It was now September 1941, and I realized that somewhere along the line I had had my twenty-first birthday, but I had no knowledge of where I had been on that great occasion, so it didn't mean very much.

Some of the activities of the camp were quite good, and over the next few months I was unable to get on a working party and had to make the best of prison life, which was not conducive to keeping very fit. Consequently I did a very rigorous course of Aikido exercises which served to keep me fit but thin.

We learned that Fort 17 was full of Russian prisoners who were being treated very badly indeed and had no Red Cross representation nor any Geneva Convention protection. They were dying off like flies and the Germans did not seem to take any measures to keep them alive.

In January 1942 I got on a transport to work on a farm which lay about an hour's train journey southeast from Torun and the journey there was very interesting.

Even the station walls had indications that spies were around with warnings like *'Feind hört mit'* – 'the enemy is listening'.

The advertisements were also of interest with cryptic questions like *'Warum ist Juno rund?'* – why are Juno (cigarettes) round?'

Everywhere on railway hoardings were pasted posters with *'Räder müssen rollen für den Sieg'* – 'wheels must turn for victory'.

The railway military police were everywhere in evidence, in their steel helmets and wearing a large crescent-shaped metal badge suspended round their necks by a chain.

There were also in evidence numerous civilians wearing black leather-belted overcoats and trilby hats, the clothes that proclaimed to all and sundry that they were Gestapo, *GEheimSTAatsPOlizei*, Secret State Police, much hated by everyone, particularly the military, and even the German guards were afraid of them.

The train seats were wooden slats, highly polished by countless bottoms and fairly primitive in construction but, old as they were, they were surprisingly comfortable, scrupulously clean and had obviously stood the test of time.

The journey was very interesting because we could see something of the way of life of the other passengers, who were nearly all women and children and were probably visiting relatives and friends in the country.

They were well muffled up with heavy overcoats and head scarves and all had baskets of food, mostly bread and sausages. Many of them wanted to give food to the prisoners but the guard absolutely forbade it so they just studied us as curiously as we studied them.

The scenery was not very inspiring; the countryside was flat, bare and covered with snow, relieved only rarely by clusters of dense conifers making up pine forests of some ten to twenty acres at a time.

Occasionally a figure was seen near a cluster of farm buildings, intent on his work and incurious about our train and its contents; he or she would be well muffled up against the cold and probably just doing odd jobs on the farm since the ground was rock-hard.

There were fifteen of us on the Arbeitskommando or working party, and only one at each farm, so obviously there was nowhere to go if one escaped, and equally the guard could not look after us all.

The arrangement was that the guard would circulate occasionally and most of the time would just telephone to the farm to ask if everything was going well with the prisoners.

At the station all our prospective bosses were waiting for us, and mine was a stoutish German with a green trilby hat with a feather in the hat band, a close-cropped fair head of hair which bristled around his fat creased neck. He sported a Hitler moustache which was de rigeur with all the civilian men; he wore a short green Austrian type of jacket, decorated on the lapels and pockets with embroidered Alpine flowers, green breeches with black *Stiefels* or jackboots.

He was fairly terse and formal and gestured me to get into the back of a farm cart while he got up into the driver's seat and whipped up the horse into a walk.

I had my kit plus a Red Cross parcel and sat wondering what lay ahead at the farm.

We journeyed on, passing a few Poles on bikes who turned round to have a look at me after we had passed so that the *Leiter*, the boss, didn't see them taking any interest.

After what seemed a very long time we came to a wooden gate and I jumped down to hold it open, while the boss drove through, then made sure to close it securely and got up on to the wagon again. We drove along a track with deep furrows and grass in the middle showing bright green tufts against the snow and presently came to a group of buildings, one of which was brick, the others being timber including some tall barns.

We went into the brick building and the German introduced himself as Hans Staub and his wife as just Frau Staub.

Frau Staub was predictably stout but quite pleasant in a motherly way and sat us both down at the kitchen table and put a large plateful of milk soup in front of us and thick slices of rye bread and ersatz butter. The milk soup was very popular on the farms because there was always enough milk and it contained little croutons of rye dough and was flavoured with just the merest touch of salt and served hot.

It was the nicest thing I had tasted for a very long time and I told the Frau this and she was obviously very pleased.

I think it was at that time that I formed the glimmering of what was to be a very productive plan.

I decided that I would work very hard indeed for this farmer, so that I could gain his confidence and as a result might be much better able to move about the countryside, make some contacts and do what I had been trained for.

Accordingly I became a farmer's lad with a zest for Arbeit, and I became stronger and stronger as the days and weeks went by.

I had a little area set aside in one of the barns where I slept; I used a little outhouse toilet which had a clean scrubbed (by me) wooden seat and a little wire ring through which were threaded large squares of newspaper and there was a plentiful supply of cut straw in a box so that it could be sprinkled down the chute after each performance.

There was also a pump, tap and trough where I washed myself each day, usually just before having the evening meal. It was an ingenious little arrangement by which one could pump the water into a tank which allowed one to have the hands free to wash or to fill a can simply by turning on the tap.

At first, in the cold weather, I was a bit appalled at washing in the open, where it was so cold that the tap had to have felt tied round it and the water pipe to stop the water freezing, and the trough into which the water ran frequently had a layer of ice in the bottom due to the dripping water from the tap.

One of the first things I did was to scrounge an old bit of leather from a discarded shoe, cut out a washer from it and put the home-made washer on the tap.

Herr Staub was quite impressed with this and after a few more little jobs like that his attitude visibly changed and he was much more communicative.

I got up just before dawn (after a while without having to be woken up) and cleaned the cows in the cowshed in preparation for milking; this entailed using a scraper on their hind quarters to scrape off all the dried dung followed by washing the udders in warm water and making sure the teats were clean and free from sores.

The cows all had their own names and their own stalls, and, in the warmer weather, when they had to be herded into their stalls, they would usually go straight in to their proper place, although sometimes a stupid one would be in the wrong stall and the rightful owner would go into the one next to it and there would be a dreadful mix-up with butting cows and cursing cowhand. This was where I learned to steer a cow where I wanted it to go by either twisting its tail (and keeping out of the way of lashing hind legs) or putting thumb and forefinger into the nostrils and just pulling or pushing it where it had to go. For the young bulls this was the safest way to guide them, before they had rings put through their noses.

When Frau Staub had cleaned the milking buckets with scalding hot water all three of us got down to the milking, putting the milk all together in big churns to take to the lane-way for collection.

During the winter months the cows stayed in the cowshed all the time, but for the rest of the year, after the milking, the cows had to be led by long chains down to a field of lucerne where I would stake them out at intervals so that they could only crop a certain amount of food in a given time; then during the day they would be shifted about two yards to give them a further area of feeding. It was a primitive but very effective way of rationing their feed.

After this, I would go to the farmhouse for first breakfast, which would be a cup of tea, clear peppermint flavoured, and slices of bread and jam. The jam was mostly ersatz but Frau Staub put other fruit in it and it did not taste too bad; I imagine that the shortage of sugar would have limited the making of proper jam.

When I first started at the farm the weather was so cold that there was no work to be done in the fields and I would spend my day cleaning harness, sharpening scythes, maintaining machinery, repairing buildings, mucking out the cowshed and generally keeping the farm operative in preparation for the coming spring when these indoor jobs had to wait for odd moments when one was not doing anything essential.

In spring, the workload increased dramatically and I was initially kept busy all day from dawn to dusk but, as I got used to the work, I became quicker at it and had some time to spare.

I would feed, water and groom the horse, harness it up and take it out to the fields that I had to plough; clean and couple up the single plough and start the horse along the furrow. I had to learn the words or sounds to get the horse to work: to start it off one had to intone in a commanding voice 'Ho rrruck' and to stop the horse 'Brrrrr' and to turn it pulling on the appropriate rein was 'Rrrroom'.

The horse knew exactly what it had to do anyway and only tried on a few variations of its own when it saw that I was inexperienced. Pretty soon, we had a good working relationship and I quite enjoyed plodding along barefooted, walking in the furrow and straining to keep the plough straight and at the required depth.

When the field was ploughed and harrowed, it was sown, usually with *Rogen* or rye, sometimes with wheat or oats, and for this we had an ancient hopper pulled along by the horse. The hopper had about ten little funnels through which the seed ran and which could be cut off by a handle at the side when we stopped, which we did frequently, to replenish the supply of seed in the hopper. At that time I handled the hundredweight sacks of seed with ease and poured the seed into the hopper from about head high.

Second breakfast would be at about eight am and we all sat down again at the kitchen table for bread and wurst, ersatz cheese, sometimes milk soup and tea.

Lunch was always eaten out on the job and would consist of sandwiches with sausage, usually liverwurst which I liked very much, with tea or coffee while the Red Cross supplies lasted, usually cold and in an empty schnapps bottle.

I made a point of sharing the Red Cross supplies with the Staub family, which was most appreciated and supplemented my plan for greater freedom of movement around the farm properties.

It was also a very useful means of propaganda because I was aware that the farmers did discuss their prisoners among themselves and I was always careful to give the impression that Britain had masses of supplies of the luxury goods in the parcels and, in particular, I noticed the wistful looks that were interchanged when I casually broke up a bar of chocolate for us to share, or handed over a beef stew for inclusion in the family soup.

All this gave the direct lie to the propaganda programs on the radio that Britain was starving because of the success of the German U-boats in maintaining a blockade of the British Isles.

The evening meal was always the best of the day and was eaten by lamplight and, when the Staubs got to know me better, particularly when they were pleased with my work, Herr Staub would bring out a bottle of Schnapps and we would sing German marching songs and sometimes I would teach them to sing British songs. It was quite incredible how many songs in English had the same tune with different words in German.

All this time I was building up the confidence of the Staubs and the guard, who originally came by twice a week, gradually lengthened this time and, in the end, he just telephoned Herr Staub whom I used to hear saying things like: 'Don't you worry about the *Rode Kopf*,[1] he is the best worker I have ever had and I treat him well and he is quite happy to stay,' and later: 'Tell the Hauptmann that the *Rode Teufel*[2] is working well and that I will be personally responsible for him if he stays here.'

Also, I was establishing a pattern of going for walks by myself, initially on the farm property and only for short times, but eventually I got to know a Pole on a neighbouring farm and was able to stay overnight on rare occasions provided always that all my work was done to the Leiter's satisfaction; which it always was, I made sure of that.

When I was sure that the Pole could be trusted, and knowing that he was not associated with the Polish Underground, I suggested to him that I was looking for a way to escape, possibly to Russia or Sweden, and that I would need some help from someone associated with the Underground. He said that he would make some enquiries and I stressed to him that he was to be careful, which was probably unnecessary because all the Poles around were born conspirators and intensely loyal to Poland; also he had been a farm worker in this district all his life and knew no other occupation, so I felt the risk was justified.

Nothing came of this immediately and I just continued in the farm life, making myself as indispensable as possible to the Staub family.

It was now July 1942 and the farm work was beginning to hot up as the time came for the main summer harvest.

It being wartime, we were having two harvests a year: the first was the winter wheat that was harvested in May, and the main summer crop that usually ripened in August.

While the corn was only knee-high or less, I would go up

---

1. Red Head
2. Red Devil

and down the furrows with a *'Distelstecker'*, which was a sort of hoe, and dig out all the weeds so that the end result at harvest time was not encumbered with thistles or poppies or any of the dozens of weeds which grew so well.

When the harvest was ready, Polish workers from the outlying farms would all descend on the one farm, with all the farm machinery available, and the harvesting would start.

I usually went behind the harvester picking up the cut corn stalks and putting them upright in stooks tied round the middle, not with string which was in short supply, but with twisted lengths of the straw which was just as good and did not need to be taken out before going into the thresher.

At that time, I would go down to all the fields, in turn and scythe the borders for about a yard in from the hedge, to allow the harvester to make a clean sweep without involving the weeds at the edge of the field.

By the time we had done all the fields, it was time to set up the threshing machine, which looked like an old caravan filled with machinery. The stooks were thrown into a hay wagon by a pitchfork and were then taken to be stacked by the side of the threshing machine.

The stooks were then pitchforked up to the roof of the thresher where someone caught them and fed them into the blades which had no safety device and were lethal if an arm accidentally got pushed in, because the owner of the arm would be pulled into the threshing blades. Consequently it was overlooked by a worker, usually an old and decrepit person, who had the responsibility of throwing a lever if there was an accident.

The corn was threshed from the straw and collected at the side of the machine where it was put into sacks, tied up and loaded on to a cart.

The straw came out of the back of the threshing machine and two unlucky individuals, with handkerchiefs over noses and mouths, had to brave the clouds of dust, chaff and straw, and pitchfork the straw into wagons where it was carefully and skilfully built up to about room high and then taken to a suitable site, usually a large barn, to be stored for the winter, when it would be used to bed down the cattle.

The corn was carted over to another barn to be stored on the upper floor, which meant that I had to carry the hundredweight sacks on my shoulder and then climb up a ladder to the opening in the barn loft and dump my sack there, where it was seized by someone else and stacked in readiness for the large lorry which would take it to the mill.

One time I was halfway up a ladder with a sack on my shoulder when someone came up the ladder behind me and goosed me.

Apart from nearly dropping the sack and risking falling off the ladder, it was a stupid thing to do and I yelled out Polish obscenities to whoever it was; I couldn't turn round to see and I couldn't kick out because of the weight of the sack, so I just yelled out more foul obscenities in Polish: '*Pierunie psiakrew ty kurwa twoja mac*' and words to that effect and continued to climb up the ladder telling him that I would really duff him up when I came down.

When I did get down I turned round and got the shock of my life; standing there with a huge grin on his face was Jan Tarasov, who had evidently found out that I was working here and had come along ostensibly to help out with the harvest but really to make contact with me.

We had a great deal to talk about and to plan, and I told him that I was very well in with the German farmer and that I could, when the work allowed, take off as much as twenty-four hours at a time if necessary, but certainly eight or nine hours at least.

My plan was to use the farm as a central safe house and to operate from there in a southwest to easterly direction, so that increased sabotage activity would appear to come from an area other than ours if it came under the scrutiny of the Germans.

I had to have a bicycle, hidden about three miles from the farm or nearer if a safe spot could be found, and then I could appear to take walks in the fields or woods as I had done for months. I could get on the bike and meet up with other partisans in agreed spots, do what we came for and then hightail it back to the farm, hide the bike and just stroll back to the farmhouse as innocently as a lamb.

Jan told me that the lad I had spoken to could be trusted because his father had been killed by the Gestapo some while ago and he worked in order to look after his mother and grandmother.

He was the one who would bring me messages, by mouth only, from Jan. It was an excellent arrangement because this time I needed no papers and could continue to wear my khaki trousers which I used for work, which were very old and worn, and had a very nondescript colour which was excellent camouflage. I had a newish uniform at the farm which I wore on Sundays, in common with the practice on these farms of wearing good clothes on Sunday (after I had done the essential chores) for greater enjoyment of the day of rest.

On a Sunday one went walking – '*spatzieren*' – although there was really nowhere to show off one's clothes; nevertheless it was the done thing and goodness knows the people there had little enough to look forward to in the week, so they made the most of Sundays.

The variety of the farm work suited me down to the ground because I had always liked to have four or five things going at the same time and that is just what farm work is all about.

Some of it was hard labour such as digging up potatoes, because, although Staub had a 'potato digger', all it really consisted of was a glorified plough which left spuds scattered over the whole field, the collecting of which was a truly back-breaking job.

Another unenviable task was the yearly harvest of sugar beet. These grow in the ground, are about nine to ten inches in their long diameter with about two or three inches of the beet showing above ground and have a luxuriant growth of green tops. One had to be armed with a large blade like a machete and, by grasping the green top, lever the beet out of the ground, hold it to one's right, slice off the greenery so that the beet drops to the ground and place the green top on the left. Thus, at the end of each row, there was a line of beet and a line of greenery. Each row would be the length of the field and coming back up, repeating the process, would leave double piles of beet and greenery which could be gathered up into a cart with a broad fork, the beet being taken to a factory for crushing and extraction of sugar, while the green tops would be put in a long earth, trench or clamp and covered over with earth progressively leaving a yard-high pile on the top of the ground extending for about five hundred yards per field of beet.

The same procedure was followed for the mangels and swedes, except that these two vegetables were kept on the farm, the mangels purely for cattle fodder but the swedes were eaten by us as well. When winter came in earnest, I would have to go out to the clamp, open up one end and take out the amount of cattle feed needed for about a week, close up the clamp again so that the frost didn't get in, and cart the fodder to the large warm cattle shed, then distribute it to the cows.

Once a week, or once a month if we were very busy, I would muck out the cowshed, remove all the dung-filled straw and make a large pile of it ready for dung-spreading in the early spring. The three or four-pronged dung fork was the heaviest item on the farm when a fork load of dung was on it, but mucking out was one of my favourite jobs in winter because it meant that I would be snug and warm in the cowshed whilst the temperature outside was well below freezing point.

The riskiest job on the farm was in the early spring when the young heifers had to be taken out and pegged down to have their first feed in the pasture land. After being cooped up all winter, they were furiously excited and bursting to go.

Each one had a wide leather collar to which was attached a ten-yard-long chain with a ring at the end. The purpose of this was to peg out each heifer twenty yards apart so that they could only eat their own little circle of lucerne or grass. The first day they had a complete semicircle from the edge of the field, but thereafter they had their pegs moved forward a yard at a time to control the feeding. Had they been allowed to roam free, they would have eaten too much and blown themselves up like balloons with the gas. If that did happen, as it did on rare occasions, then I had to stick a metal tube into their side to deflate them; and, in fact, they did go down just like a deflated balloon with the gas hissing out of the tube and making a really foul smell. The little hole in their side was then covered with pitch and soon healed.

I made the mistake once of taking eight of the heifers out at one time and one of them ran ahead of me followed by another and before I could do anything I was encircled by chains and at very real risk of being squeezed to death. Fortunately, I was able to drop the chains and to disentangle myself from them, whilst the exuberant heifers careered all over the field.

Hay making was quite an interesting job and very easy. All I had to do was to scythe a field of grass when it was about a foot high; scything is a very rhythmic and good exercise and easy once you get the hang of keeping the tip of the blade clear of the ground. A good farmhand can scythe a fair sized field, say four or five acres, in one day without too much effort. Sometimes we had a co-operative effort with the cutting; there would be six of us in a diagonal line, all scything in time and taking a step forward with each stroke in a sort of ballet of movement, with the singing hiss of the blades keeping time.

Once the hay was cut it had to be turned a couple of times, and after about a week the horse was harnessed up to the hay rake and I just had to sit on a sack on the iron seat and drive around raking up the hay into lines by means of a lever at my side which raised and lowered the rake.

When this was done the horse was harnessed on to a hay wagon and as it walked down between the lines all on its own, two of us would pitchfork the hay into the wagon.

When the wagon was piled really high it was taken back to a spot near the cowsheds and a haystack was made measuring about six yards square, with the hay packed so that the stalks were always on the outside and sloping down to make the stack less permeable to rain, snow and frost.

Towards the end, we were standing on sticks stuck into the side of the stack; and, in this way, we could throw the hay up the side of the stack, passing it from one pitchfork to the next up to as high as twenty feet. The reason for such a huge stack was something to do with the cold but I never could understand just what that was.

Chapter 7

1942

While all this was going on I was taking my customary stroll around the place, to which everyone was well accustomed.

Because I was such a good worker they all put up with this little idiosyncrasy, and I believe that some thought I was pro German in my eagerness and obvious dedication to work for work's sake.

The surrounding countryside was extremely isolated and there existed only a few tracks along which to ride the bike, but it was certainly quicker than walking.

Some twenty kilometres to the south, there was a main road running east and west which carried only military traffic and mostly large convoys of ammunition and tanks and was generally packed with trucks of German soldiers.

On many occasions, we did counts of the traffic and sent back the information to Britain via the Polish Underground.

The convoy would usually be led by a small scout car with an officer, a Feldwebel and a driver. Eighty to a hundred yards back would be a truck containing troops, then a heavy transport vehicle with either a heavy gun or a tank, then a truck of soldiers, then an anti-aircraft truck, then anything and finally a heavy aid truck to handle any breakdowns.

Outriders on motorcycles, either solo or combination machines with a sidecar, very similar to the 650 cc Nortons that we had trained with in England, would accompany the more important convoys, driving ahead and blocking side tracks or crossroads so that the convoy was not held up by farm wagons or slower vehicles.

The intervals between vehicles were always rigidly observed and were around the hundred yards mark and never less than sixty yards.

Occasionally the Feldwebel would get out of the scout car and stand by the roadside to check that the intervals were observed. Should any driver be too close to the truck in front, he would be noted and probably punished when the convoy reached its destination.

German army discipline is the strictest in the world and during training the officers and non-commissioned ranks often knock the trainees around physically by kicking them, slapping their faces or pushing them into the ground. This is condoned and even applauded by their commanders and produces an army which instantly obeys all commands without question and consequently ranks among the finest in the world.

I had been asked to advise about the destruction of some of these vehicles and we had decided that the best way was with mines.

Accordingly, we used three large and thirty smaller anti-personnel mines, the latter being quite small and handy and only powerful enough to blow a leg off or the wheel off a vehicle. The big ones would each take out a whole truck and toss it into the air like a matchbox.

We had to try to set the mines a short distance around a bend and bends were not very frequent in that road. However, even if we went quite a distance away from our area, the disadvantage was balanced by the fact that we were operating a greater distance from our base and there was that extra degree of safety.

We chose an S-bend and placed the leading mine about thirty yards beyond the last bend.

The road was furrowed with the constant traffic and it was noted that the heavy vehicles kept to these furrows whereas the light scout cars kept to the centre piece between the furrows.

Consequently, we placed one of the big mines in the middle section of the road where the scout car tyres would strike it, and the second big one fifty yards back in the right hand furrow, hopefully to collect the front wheel of the big transporter.

The personnel mines were placed another fifty yards back, but by the side of the road so that any troops descending from their vehicle to see what the hold up was, would probably set off a few of them. They were laid in fours at fifty yards intervals, two on each side of the road, or sometimes three on the left and one on the right.

The third big mine was placed about a mile further on so that either the subsequent clean-up sweep would miss it or, if they found it, they would have to sweep the road for a considerable distance ahead, which would effectively close the road to traffic for some time.

The expectation was that the scout car and the first truck would be hit and that the convoy would stop.

Almost certainly the commanders in the following vehicles would descend to see what was happening, probably being careful to avoid the road surface and hopefully encountering the personnel mines by the roadside.

In fact this is roughly what did happen, except that the officer in command was killed in the scout car and another, presumably the second-in-command, must have thought that this was an attack by partisans because he gave the order for the troops to get out of the trucks and spread out around the convoy, thus causing far greater troop destruction than would have been the case had the men remained in their vehicles.

At the time it happened everyone concerned in the laying was long gone.

The road was out of commission for quite a while.

There was also a railway further south which carried long

trains of weapons, troops and vehicles; this had all the appearances of an attractive target.

The times of trains varied and so did the freight they carried and it was obvious that we would have to use the plastic explosive wired to a detonator and operated by someone nearby with a view of the train.

We chose a hill about half a mile from the track and laid the wire carefully all the way to a spot about twenty yards from the rail, by a small pine tree. This main wire was covered over by a layer of the sandy soil and was quite safe from discovery.

The track itself was a different matter because it was inspected frequently, at random times, by a linesman who would be driven fairly slowly along in a funny little skeleton truck propelled by a rocking lever. He would stop every now and then and hit the rail with a steel hammer, and it was obvious that he knew what he was doing and couldn't be relied on to miss anything suspicious.

We finally decided on a plan whereby an observer would signal by radio when a suitable train was coming and we would have ten minutes approximately to set the explosive, wire up to the main wire twenty yards away, and get the hell out of the area before the train came.

We had a dummy run and decided that ten minutes was time enough and that the person setting the charge should escape to the south so that subsequent investigations would show footprints going in that direction rather than to the north, where the one connecting the battery to detonate the plastic would have to dig a hole beforehand to dump the battery and, if possible, pull in the wire and dump that as well and bury them.

In the event, there were three sets of footprints going south and the blast effectively covered all the tracks to the north and the wire was successfully pulled in and buried; so the whole job went off very well except that no real intelligence came back about the contents of the trucks blown up, only that they were effectively disabled for a long time and that the locomotive was a write-off.

I did hear that a number of Poles were shot as a result of the derailment but this happened all the time whenever anything went wrong for the Germans and it was accepted as a risk of war and just served to make the Poles more determined than ever to get rid of as many Germans as they could.

Throughout the whole of 1942 it was quite a common sight to see Red Cross train-loads of German soldiers returning from the *'Schwerer kampfen im Osten'*, the heavy fighting on the Eastern Front.

The daily papers had whole pages of lists of missing and killed and it became quite obvious that the Germans had suffered a major setback, if not a downright defeat, on the Russian Front.

There was really no way in which they could fight in the Russian winter and as the offensive, intended to be a Blitzkrieg or 'lightning war' named Operation Barbarossa, gradually came to a halt, so the supplies slowed down and there was much less activity of troop movement than there had been in the preceding six months.

I think 1942 was the year the Germans realized they were not invincible.

Life for me went on in much the same way and by now I was fairly well established in my farm job and in touch with most of the local Underground.

I was quite surprised at how many of the Poles, especially the womenfolk, were doing work for the Partisans and the Underground.

The German Gestapo made no distinction between women and men in the punishment they dished out and after each success of the Underground they would at this time shoot Poles they probably believed to be innocent and hang anyone publicly they caught red-handed. In each case the punishment would follow intensive 'interrogation', which was really aggressive torture, unrefined brutality, so that the final execution was probably longed-for and welcome.

Those who were hanged would be strung up in a public

place with a cardboard notice attached to their bodies front and back indicating that this was the punishment for killing German soldiers.

The jobs we did were aimed to slow down the German war effort but they were very small compared to those of the Partisans, whose job was essentially armed resistance, a constant hit and run, relying on local knowledge to dodge the inevitable retaliation from the Wehrmacht. In this way, a substantial force had to be maintained to enable the Germans to protect their lines of communication and transport to the Eastern Front.

Our efforts were occasionally explosive but more often a subtle erosion of the German war effort.

'Räder müssen rollen für den Sieg', but it was difficult to get wheels to roll when fine sand had been mixed with the wheel grease.

String was an innocent enough object, but when soaked in salt petre and allowed to dry it became a useful fuse to commit acts of arson and general destruction on a minor scale.

Precious petrol was used for important transport purposes only and, when mixed with a little precious Red Cross sugar, it was a totally destructive agent in a petrol engine, many of which seized up completely.

Small acts, but when added up and multiplied, they had to have a drag effect on the Germans, who became very paranoid about every bit of bad luck they had and were looking under every stone for non-existent snakes.

By the end of 1942, with America coming into the war and with the Eastern Front a bit of a stalemate, the mood of the Germans did begin to change, so that they were not quite so certain that they were going to win the war. Their confidence suffered a few blows with the counter propaganda revealing failures where before they had only heard about successes.

Nevertheless the determination to force a victory was still very much in evidence and the troop morale was still excellent.

However, it was not possible to conceal the awful toll on manpower at the Eastern Front; one saw constantly the soldiers with arms and legs amputated and with scars and wounds and with the loss of sight and so on; this, more than anything, made the civilian population realize that the war was not going as well as the propaganda would have one believe.

By May 1943 news filtered through that the Germans had been pushed out of North Africa.

This was a major defeat which could not be shrugged off by the German propaganda machine because the returned soldiers themselves spread the word about their crushing defeat at Tunis and the lack of supplies from Germany to keep them going during the African campaign.

News of all this was put about by the civilian population and did a great deal of harm to the German war effort.

In May 1943 the farm work was going very steadily and, since this time of the year was not very busy, we decided that we would 'do in' a powerhouse substation which had a large transformer and a whole series of cables associated with it and was of great importance to the civilian and military authorities.

I had not had any training in the destruction of this type of installation and was doubtful that we could make the best use of our supply of plastic explosive. However, it was clearly a very desirable target and we decided to have a go at it.

Access was not a problem as we got hold of two keys which fitted the primitive lock; actually a bent nail was all that we needed to unlock this but it was quicker with the key.

Opportunity was provided by the rather lax guarding of the installation and the regular breaks that the guards had. Also, the guards went off duty at about five in the afternoon, and we were able to have a free run of the place from then until seven o'clock in the morning.

We planned to attack the actual windings on the transformer in the hope that the unbridled power would form a solid fusion effect by a weld from the sparks.

I was completely vague on this but one of the Poles was an electrician and, as I understood it, the essential of the transformer was to cut down a massive current to a number of different sub-cables which would distribute the reduced current to a number of utilities using electricity.

It seemed sensible therefore to attack the most powerful current for the maximum effect.

We had to unbolt the casing of the transformer, which bore horrific signs of skull and crossbones and lightning flashes, indicating that inside the casing was death. So we put the plastic against the inside of the metal case, keeping our grubby little fingers off the contents, and re-bolted the casing tightly, burring the thread against any nosy inspection and leading the very fine detonating wire out of sight and into the ground and under the door hinge, then out of the compound to a convenient spot for attachment to a longer cable which could be used to detonate the plastic from a relatively safe distance and allow the one who did the detonating to pull in the wire and bury the battery and wire so that there would be no evidence available.

This was one job where we could not know what precisely would happen when the balloon went up and we were not keen to be around when it did.

I decided that I would not be on the scene for this one, but would have an alibi by being on the farm and being seen to be there at the time of the explosion. I don't know whether I had some premonition about this one but I was not very happy about the nearness of the objective to the farm nor the unpredictable effects of the explosion.

I rode back on the bike and hid it in the usual place under a pile of old dead branches in a ditch by a hedge about a mile from the farm boundary. I walked back to the farmhouse without being seen by anyone.

The detonation was scheduled for three o'clock in the morning and that evening I made a point of letting Herr Staub know that I was feeling a bit off with diarrhoea and vomiting and I went without any food that evening, which was very unusual for me and made the Frau a bit anxious too. Actually I did have a lot of butterflies in the stomach so going without food was no hardship.

I was in bed by eight o'clock and an hour later Herr Staub looked in to see how I was and to ask if he should phone the guard. I told him that I would be alright in the morning and thanked him for his kindness.

At three in the morning there was an almighty explosion which woke everyone up and I went into the farmhouse to ask what was the matter: — *Was ist los, Herr Staub? — Russische Flieger, vielleicht; wie geht's mit dem Bauch? — Besser, danke. Aber muss man weiter schlafen gehen.*

(What's the matter, Herr Staub ? — Russian planes, perhaps; how's the stomach ? — Better, thanks. But I think I'd better get some more sleep.)

After this brief exchange to establish my presence I went back to my room and lay thinking about the explosion. It had sounded very much too loud, so presumably the charge had been excessive in relation to the target. Then I thought that the reason could be that the cast-iron casing was stronger than it had looked and that would act as a counter-compressant increasing the explosion and causing a shrapnel effect.

It was not long before dawn and I decided that I would get up early and do some of the many little jobs on a farm that get put off until there is a lull in activity. Things like cutting chaff on the ancient but effective cutting machine that I had oiled and sharpened with such loving care so that it no longer let out agonized rusty squeaks when turning the handle.

I also sharpened the scythes and put some grease on the blades before wrapping them up in sacking.

All the time I was subconsciously listening for sounds of approaching cars indicating the arrival of the Gestapo.

I hammered out the ends of the shovel on an ancient anvil, straightened the tines on the dung fork, which had five tines to the pitchfork's two.

Finally, I started mucking out the cowshed which was an enjoyable task with the warm sweet smell of the cows breath and the not unpleasant smell of the dung and straw.

The dung was about a foot deep and needed to be heaved by fork to the entrance of the shed and then heaved again from the entrance to the dung heap. In order to lift the forkful of dung, one had to use the hip as a fulcrum and lever the fork against it, otherwise it was impossible to lift up the dung.

Some farmers used to let the dung in the cowshed mount up during the fiercely cold winters so that the level was raised to about a yard. The reason for this was that the dung acted as a kind of central heating and was constantly trampled down by the cattle so that all that was needed each morning was to put down a fresh layer of straw. The cows were always very well looked after in the winter because it was so nice to be able to get warm, and the metal scraper was used to scrape off the dried dung from the cow's hide, then a stiff wire brush cleaned off the rest of the hide and the cow's coat would be shining once again.

The cows loved it and also loved to be spoken to whenever one was in the shed. During all my contact with the cows I never once came across a bad one and was never ever kicked or stamped on by them. Cows have the most beautiful eyes with long lashes and are really lovely animals to which one could get quite attached after working with them for a while.

That day went very slowly and I had to reassure Herr Staub that I was feeling fit again, so maybe some of the strain was showing.

In the afternoon, he had three telephone calls, which was unusual in itself, and at the evening meal he told me that a big electrical installation had been blown up by terrorists and that the Gestapo had arrived in force and were questioning everyone in the area.

They both looked very worried at the prospect and were scared stiff of the secret police as were all German civilians. They all had stories to tell about the torture and interrogation of innocent people by the Gestapo and the type of punishment for things like defeatist talk, for expressing doubt about the Hitler regime or for expressing any kind of sympathy for the Jews or concern at the process of their elimination.

Although a great many of the civilian population were aware of the extermination camps and the policy of a clean Aryan race without any Zionist pollution, yet they spoke very little about it and professed to know nothing or to say that they, the Germans, were only the 'little people' who should not get involved with politics and that anyway the Jews were not people but just Jews and getting rid of them was right and proper.

The fact was that, between the Gestapo and the war propaganda of Dr Goebbels, the German people were trapped, and they knew that, if they did not go along with the propaganda, they would attract the attention of the Gestapo and land up in trouble.

Chapter 8

1943

Two days after the explosion, at about noon, a black Mercedes drew up outside the farmhouse and two men got out.

They stood looking around at everything and appeared in no hurry to go into the house.

One was shortish with a pale fat face and thick horn-rimmed spectacles; he wore a black Homburg type of trilby, had a black overcoat, black trousers and black shoes. The other one was taller, leaner and younger. He wore a dark trilby and a longish black leather overcoat, belted and with large patch pockets.

When they had surveyed the area they went, in a leisurely fashion, to the farmhouse door and, without knocking, walked in.

They were indoors with the Staubs for about an hour and then Herr Staub came out and called me into the house.

We went into a sort of front parlour that was almost never used, where the two men were sitting down comfortably at ease with Frau Staub sitting on an upright chair, right on the edge of the seat, looking very scared indeed.

Herr Staub said to me: "These gentlemen are from the

State Police and they want to ask you a few questions." With that both Staub and his wife got up and left the room.

The short fat one opened the conversation. "Herr Staub tells me that you are a good worker."

I said: "I'm sorry but I do not speak more than a little German. Would you please say that again more slowly?"

He said: "*Du gut Arbeiter, ja?*" (You're a good worker, yes?)

I said: "*Ja gut Arbeiter.*"

He said: "*Warum Kriegsgefangener arbeitet so gut?*" (Why should a prisoner of war work so well?)

I said: "*Ich liebe Bauernarbeit.*" (I like farm work)

"*Was has du für Regiment?*" (What's your Regiment?)

"*Bitte?*" (Pardon?)

"*Name von Regiment?*" (The name of your Regiment?)

"*Sechs acht neun sechs drei sechs drei.*" (6896363)

"*Nein, DER NAME!*" (Getting a bit cross now and shouting)

"Jack Martin Goyder, *achtundsechzigneun dreiundsechzig dreiundsechzig.*" (6896363)

"*NEIN, REGIMENTSNAME, REGIMENTSNAME!!*"

"*Nicht verstehen.*" (I don't understand)

The younger one said: "We are wasting our time with this one. We'll take him in for questioning and get an interpreter."

To me he said: "*Komm mit.*" (Come along)

We went out to the car and I was put in the back seat with the younger man and the fat one got in the front and we drove off. I remember seeing a tearful Frau Staub with her hand holding a handkerchief to her mouth standing at the farmhouse door watching us go.

We drove very quickly for about three -quarters of an hour and pulled up at some scattered buildings where we went straight into a house and down into a room at the basement, where there was a desk and three chairs and a filing cabinet and a large bulb in a small light socket with a green shade and a pulley arrangement to alter the height of the light.

I sat in the chair for about twenty minutes while the fat one looked through some papers on his desk.

Presently the door opened and a very thin Gefreiter in faded uniform came in with the younger man and stood as stiffly to attention as his stooping shoulders would allow. The younger man stood by my side.

This was a more formal interrogation and the Gefreiter was an interpreter with a slight American accent.

"Name?"

"Jack Martin Goyder."

"Prisoner of war number?"

"8136."

"Stalag?"

"XXa."

"Where did you get the bicycle from?" This was meant to be a surprise question but I had warning via the interpreter, although the fat one was speaking in very fast German to the interpreter.

"What bicycle?"

"The one you rode on the farm."

"I didn't have a bicycle on the farm, I always walked. I love walking."

"We have witnesses who saw you riding the bicycle."

"They are mistaken, I rode no bicycle." I had always been very careful that no one should see me on the bike and I was pretty certain that they were bluffing me.

"You are lying. We can prove that you have ridden the bicycle."

"I am not lying. I am a British prisoner of war and I am under the protection of the Geneva Convention and the German Wehrmacht."

Whoops. It was probably this last statement that pushed them too far; I finished up on the floor not knowing what had hit me but with a loud ringing in both ears. It had obviously been the young Gestapo agent standing by my side, because he was yelling at me that saboteurs had no protection from anyone, and he grabbed me and pulled me back on to the chair.

The fat one smiled with his mouth only and said: "Why do

you not confess that you have been associated with some subversive Polish terrorists who have forced you to help them? We do not believe that you helped them willingly and all we need is some identification of the Poles and we will return you to your Stalag."

"If I knew anything I would certainly help you. All I want to do is to last out to the end of the war and then go home to England."

"You will think about helping us to find the gangsters who have been sabotaging the German Reich. You will be interrogated again."

With that the three Germans left the room, leaving me to my misery. Almost at once the door opened and an SS guard in uniform motioned me to go out and took me down the road to the Police Station and I was locked up in a cell.

There was a straw palliasse on the floor and a bucket in the corner with an old newspaper. The small barred window was too high to see out of and, in any case, I was not interested in viewing the scenery. The most humiliating part of all this came in a few minutes when two guards came in to my cell and put my ankles in metal handcuffs which bit into the skin and only allowed me to shuffle around like an old-time convict. I protested that it was not necessary but the guard told me it was orders, shrugged his shoulders and left it at that. The trouble was that it caused leg ulcers even in the few days that I had it and the ulcers took many weeks to heal up.

I spent the rest of the day on the palliasse with no food or water and the night was pretty cold and very long.

In the morning they brought me half a rye loaf and a metal water bottle, military issue.

By noon I had had a bit more sleep and was feeling more optimistic when they escorted me out of the cell and into one of the rooms.

The interrogation followed much the same lines as the previous day, starting with the same questions and answers, except that the knocking about by the younger Gestapo was more in evidence, while the fat one appeared to be restraining his colleague and trying to give me the impression that he was sympathetic towards me.

We covered the ground of the farm work and the opportunities I would have had to slip away from the farm, the contacts I could have made, the sabotage I could have done.

All this I denied vigorously, asserting my innocence and trying to give the impression of righteous indignation and horror at their treatment of an innocent prisoner of war.

"How many Poles were there?"

"I wasn't there so I don't know."

THUMP!!

On the floor again, my ears were ringing and my neck was hurting and there was a sense of unreality about the whole thing.

The questions seemed to come from a long way away and I felt nauseated and faint.

"Describe one of the Poles."

"It little profits that an idle king,
By this still hearth, among these barren crags,
Matched with an aged wife, I mete and dole
Unequal laws unto a savage race
That hoard and sleep and feed and know not me."

Snatches of verses learnt at school came flooding into my head and I was saying them out loud.

To hell with these bastards.

"Interpreter, what is he saying?"

"Something about a wife, Mein Herr."

"Describe one of the women."

"Of Nelson and the North,
Sing the glorious days renown.
When to battle fierce came forth
All the might of Denmark's crown."

"I do not understand, Mein Herr, he is making no sense."

"Just tell me what he says, you fool."

"He talks of fighting for a Danish krone."

"You swine, you are wasting our time."

THUMP!!

It seemed to make very little difference what I said, I still got beaten up, but hopefully they would think I was going a bit mad and that might make them give up.

The interpreter had obviously not had the benefit of a classical education so the next day after the beatings started I quoted a bit of Virgil's Aeneid, as much as anything to give myself a mental boost that I was not going to break down. 'Conticuere omnes intentique ora tenebant . . . ' (All hushed intent and every face turned rapt towards him)

It had a very soothing effect on me and I repeated this first line over and over out loud.

It did give me a bit of a respite from the thumping, but in the end I don't think I was fully with it, because I do not remember getting back to the cell.

I had about a week of this, by which time I was pretty well done in and, on the sixth or seventh day, I was joined in my cell by a Pole they had knocked about in a similar fashion, to judge by his appearance. They just heaved him into the cell in the early afternoon and threw in a palliasse after him.

For a long time he was quiet and then he looked up at me with a rueful grin; and said something in Polish which I did not understand. When I shrugged my shoulders, he said in very poor German that they had accused him of blowing up a signal box; and that he had helped some of his friends to do this; and that they were trying to get him to tell them the names of his friends but he would not do so.

He also told me, in a very confidential way, that he had been responsible for a number of acts of sabotage in Poland which the Germans knew nothing about. A little later he asked me if I was in the same trouble.

Remembering my old instructor's advice to trust no one, I replied that I had simply been working on a farm when these two Gestapo agents had arrested me for no reason at all, and were trying to make me confess to all sorts of crimes that I would never dream of doing, nor would I know the first thing about sabotage and that it was all very unfair to accuse me just because they found a bicycle on the same farm where I worked.

The Pole was sympathetic and said that, in his case, he would probably be shot on suspicion whereas the British soldiers were treated much better.

It was at this stage that I was convinced that he was a plant by the Germans to try to get me to say that I had been involved with the Polish saboteurs; so, regardless of what he added, I stuck to the same story of total innocence.

In the morning, he was taken out for further interrogation and I never saw him again.

Two days later, an army truck came by and I was handed over to the Wehrmacht, driven back to Stalag 13a and put in the bunker for two weeks.

At the end of this time, I was sent to a camp at a place called Falkenberg where I was put in a section with other prisoners of different nationalities who had given the authorities some trouble.

In the other sections, separated from us by barbed wire, were other very thin and emaciated men and women in striped uniforms with large round patches on the back; these unfortunates spent the whole time leaning against the wire begging for any scraps of food.

I realized that this was a concentration camp and that the stripers were either Jews or political prisoners.

Once a week we went into the delousers and I realized just how the poor wretches felt going into the gas chambers.

The drill was very similar to all the other delousers through which I had passed and I suppose was standard throughout the country and occupied territories.

The familiar routine of undressing and bundling up our clothes, having our hair clipped off all over, passing under a spray like a car wash, except that this one was well laced with carbolic and we learned to keep our eyes screwed up tight and our mouths shut. Into the shower proper, cold, of course, well, there was a war on. Rubbing ourselves with the abrasive soap and finally drying with the equally abrasive ersatz towels, the drying-up cloths filled with spiky bits of straw which had escaped the softening process, and gave one nasty little grazes and scratches in the more tender parts of the anatomy.

All clean and shiny, we emerged into the final room to collect our bundle of clothes and get dressed.

We were given one loaf between ten daily, a soup made of water and swedes, about half a pint, collected in mess tins or any other tins we could scrounge, as much water as we could drink and absolutely nothing else.

Red Cross parcels never reached this camp while I was there; there were no little jobs to earn extra food, no guards to chat up, nothing to do except long for the next meal and wonder how long we could hang out.

I was one of the lucky ones in that I had started very fit, well fed and strong. Most of the others had been roughing it on the run and were thin and emaciated as were the poor wretches in the other compounds. Tuberculosis was rife in these compounds and some happy releases were obtained by contracting tuberculous meningitis which generally resulted in about five days of screaming and yelling fits and then the longed-for death.

After a month, I was sent back to Stalag XXa, outside Graudenz, and it was like moving into a luxury hotel.

My little bundle of kit was there waiting for me, with letters and personal parcels from home, Red Cross parcels, proper meals, one loaf between three, potatoes as well as swedes in the soup, ersatz butter and honey, acorn coffee when the Red Cross real coffee ran out. Life was indeed looking good.

I spent a lot of time writing to everyone at home, and assuring them that I was being well looked after, and expected to be home for Christmas. This was standard ploy because we all firmly believed that the folks at home required reassurance that we would be back soon and we never said which Christmas it would be.

I had applied for a working party but was told that I would not be allowed to go out of the camp so I had to make the best of a bad job inside.

Therefore I tried to settle down to the life inside the barbed wire, where we were a community apart from the outside world.

At this time the British prisoners of war were receiving Red Cross parcels on a regular basis and also personal parcels from their families and friends in the United Kingdom.

Consequently, they were no longer the starving, scrounging characters of a few years ago. Then it had been a common sight to see a party of prisoners, half-a-dozen unkempt men, slouching along the side of the street with eyes on the ground, searching for cigarette or cigar ends thrown down by the more prosperous civilians. They would be accompanied by a German guard who looked and behaved like a soldier.

Sometimes a civilian would gesture to the guard with a packet of sandwiches, and, if the guard nodded permission, the civilian would hand the packet to the prisoners.

Now it was a complete reversal where the half-dozen prisoners would be smartly and warmly dressed, marching along briskly in step, being followed, sometimes with difficulty, by an unkempt guard whose field-grey uniform had seen better days and was really too thin to keep out the bitterly cold winds; whose step was often a limp from a war wound, or who was just too old to keep up with the group of relatively young and active prisoners.

In these times, the morale of the prisoners was excellent and, in the country work parties, when the guard was good to the prisoners, he would be looked after by them to the extent that he would be supplied with cigarettes and chocolate. In exchange he would allow the prisoners to do only as much work as they wanted.

I have seen a party of prisoners, out in the wilds, helping an aged guard back to their camp, one prisoner carrying his rifle and another his haversack, while the poor old guard stumbled along with a bad leg, possibly from a war wound, maybe even a wound from the First World War, or maybe the old joints were arthritic, quite unfit to guard anyone, but well looked after by the prisoners so that they could keep him in charge of them and do what they liked on the job.

Some of the prisoners were getting a bit cheeky towards the guards and taking quite a number of risks in the process.

One such was a Cockney called Smudger Smith, who reckoned he knew all the answers and used to show off to the other prisoners by baiting some of those guards who understood English and were sent into the compound to try to hear whether tunnels were being built or escapes planned.

They were called snoopers and many other things besides, and were considered by Smudger to be fair game.

He would go up to one of them, a naive individual called Heinrich Muller, who had one mission in life which was to convert the prisoners to the German ways and beliefs.

"Wotcha, Heinie, how's the Fuhrer today?"

"Ze Fuhrer iss, as alvays, ferry vell, Schmidt."

"And how is the Luftwaffe?"

"Ze Cherman Eagle iss flying over England each day and making life zere ferry bad for Schurchill."

"May the German Eagle spread its wings!"

"Ja, ja, Schmidt, may ze Cherman Eagle schpread its vings!"

Then, in a loud voice, Smudger and a group of his pals would chant in chorus: "May the German Eagle spread its wings!" twice more and little Heinrich would join in, delighted that he had finally converted a group of English Tommies, and fairly dribbling in his excitement, only to have his hopes dashed to the ground as Smudger said once more, "may the German Eagle spread its wings and split its bleedin' arse'ole".

All the prisoners had regained their self-respect and confidence and this was demonstrated by the many activities now undertaken in the main prison camps.

Concert parties, which were really theatre groups, had sprung up and were flourishing, thanks to the undoubted talents of many of the prisoners. In fact, a number of these actors did succeed in making a career in the theatre and in films after the war and one such, Sammy Kydd, appeared in dozens of films, in minor character roles, for many years.

The productions at this time were quite professional and

well-known plays were enacted, such as the Aldwych farces written by Ben Travers and acted, in London, by the team including Ralph Lynn, Tom Walls, Robertson Hare and Mary Brough who, before the war, had huge successes with such plays as 'Rookery Nook' and 'A Cuckoo in the Nest' to the degree that they appeared in films of the same name and almost every one of the prisoners was familiar with them.

A group of prisoners also wrote, produced and acted in comic operettas, created from snatches of familiar music (one didn't have to worry about copyright in this situation) to which the libretto was adapted so as to produce some very funny and entertaining situations. This talented group called themselves 'Gags Unlimited' and contained prisoners from all walks of life, including musicians and pictorial artists.

One must remember that few of the prisoners were professional soldiers, so that there was a sprinkling of talent and experience covering most occupations.

Costumes for the theatre productions were made by tailors from materials smuggled in by the guards in exchange for Red Cross items of food and cigarettes, and these dresses and suits were professionally made for each production and stored in rooms in the main camps.

Make-up was obtained officially through the Red Cross or the German Wehrmacht.

A band was formed of amateur and professional musicians. This orchestra obtained instruments through the Germans or the Red Cross, had regular rehearsals and achieved a really professional standard.

Stages were built, curtains made, often from blankets, stage sets and theatre wings and back-drops were made and painted by artists. Stage lighting was set up by electricians and the end result was a production that would not have disgraced a regular repertory company in civilian life.

There was also none of the usual inhibitions necessary in the theatre proper so that some of the words added to music were a bit raw but never downright coarse.

An example of the script content is provided by a Christmas

pantomime, 'Cinderella', where a large frog footman, played by Norman Freebury, was resplendent in tails and very tight breeches, standing outside a large entrance door. Cinderella and escort come along and stop by the door.

The escort speaks to the footman:

"Can you tell me where the ballroom is ?"

The footman bends both knees, clutches his groin in agony and says: "Sorry, Cock, there ain't no ballroom 'ere."

The female impersonators were generally slim and good-looking youngsters, very brave to have taken such a part which inevitably resulted in a lot of leg-pulling and ridicule from the troops in general. Their fellow actors were always very protective, often needlessly, because some of the female impersonators were tough characters. On reflection, one would have to be fairly tough to play the part of a pretty girl amongst a few hundred men who had not spoken to a female for some years.

The German guards and the officers in charge of them were always invited to the first nights and sat in the front row obviously thoroughly enjoying themselves, probably smoking English cigarettes which may have been bartered for some of the materials for the costumes in the play.

It was noticeable that the British prisoners really had the situation well controlled, as far as the Germans were concerned. We had the food, chocolate and cigarettes with which to barter and to bribe the guards, so that it was not surprising that all sorts of goods found their way into the camp including cameras, radios, bottles of schnapps and so on, all strictly forbidden, but smuggled in by the guards in exchange for chocolate, soap or cigarettes.

This was a complete reversal of the time, a few years back, when the prisoners were exchanging their watches, rings and other personal valuables for bread.

It was the Germans who were now short of food and unable to get such luxuries as chocolate or real soap, and it was the prisoners who were profiting by gaining control of the guards to the extent that, should a new guard arrive who started to shout or to threaten the prisoners, that guard would find himself posted to an area where he could exercise no influence on the POWs, such as the tower duties, where he would be stuck up in a raised tower overlooking the compound, wearing straw boots over his uniform boots, in an effort to keep warm, stamping around all day doing nothing.

There were now books available, musical instruments to learn, language courses, lectures, talks, hobbies, boxing, football and many other activities.

But always within the confines of the barbed wire.

There were ingeniously planned escapes, some successful, some ending in the sheepish return to the Stalag, some ending in an announcement by the German Kommandant that the escapee had been shot dead. The latter always brought home to us the true situation, that we were at war with the Germans, and not just being looked after by them for the duration.

After pestering the Kommandant's office and telling them that I had been wrongly accused by the Gestapo, and there being no love lost between the Wehrmacht and the Gestapo, I finally managed to get on a working party within the suburbs of Graudenz by pretending that I was a brickie.

So, once again, I was able to get out to work and get extra food, exercise and all the little extra benefits that work outside the camp entailed.

I got a lot of help from one of the other brickies, who had done this in civvy street, a little runt of a man, a Geordie from Morpeth near Newcastle. He was a foul-mouthed little bloke from the slums of his town but he had a heart of gold and, as I was a quick learner, and had done a bit of bricklaying in another working party near Graudenz as a civilian, he taught me quickly the rudiments of bricklaying so that I was able to satisfy the German civilian *Obermeister* and I became quite interested in the work.

We were building a large barrack complex designed to house army troops and it was two storeys high, fairly typical of barracks the world over. We started the first few courses under direct supervision of the civilian boss who was an Austrian, fat, hearty, red-faced, with the inevitable Hitler moustache and close-cropped hair (as we all had, it was de rigueur in this war). He wore black *Stiefels*, the shiny black military boots worn by most German males, and green breeches with a natty little green jacket that was decorated with braided patterns and had a green velvet collar. The whole effect was topped off with a green alpine trilby with a tufted feather (green, by the way) in the hat band.

He had a wooden ruler, permanently attached to his right hand, and he measured everything in sight.

The name of the suburb in Graudenz was Neueheimat, New Home, so we were, in a way, starting a new community and we wanted to be sure that it did us credit.

To this end, I spent a lot of time with Geordie discussing the types of lime, cement and sand proportions, and finding out what would happen if the proportions were not correct.

Apparently, the results of bad mixtures were utterly disastrous to a two-storey building, whether or not girders or beams were used, because the weight distribution eventually relied on the integrity of the cement used as a mortar.

This was new to me and I was quite excited about it because it meant that we had the responsibility of ensuring that the building would not fall down, when occupied, merely by the fact that we had to ensure the right proportions of lime and cement to the sand.

Cement added to sand still looks like cement because it colours the whole mixture, so the quantity of cement added is very difficult to detect visually and the added lime makes little or no difference to the colour. Of course, a brickie would spot the difference at once because the inherent 'stickiness' and 'slip' of the mortar mix would be lost; but we were the brickies, weren't we?

Next, we had to consider the points of the building which would take the brunt of the weight and the stresses and strains.

I am sure that the Austrian and the foreman were most

impressed by the care and thought that the two Englander brickies put into their work, walking round and pointing to the various areas of the building. It gave the Germans great confidence to know that their barracks to be were so carefully constructed. So much so, that they left much of the work to us, merely referring to the plans from time to time to ensure that we were following the right route, and checking the weekly quantities of material used instead of the daily quantities.

In certain areas, where stresses were greatest, because breeze blocks were not invented, or at least not apparently used, it was the practice to put up wooden shuttering, stick some metal rods inside of it, then fill the shuttering with concrete. This provided a much stronger wall than the bricks and mortar, but it was important, not only to get the mixture right, but to ensure that no cement bags or rubbish found its way into the shuttering with the concrete; otherwise the walls would, in time, crumble.

Chapter 9

1944

Neueheimat was a saboteur's dream and with judicious mixing of the various ingredients we reckoned that the barracks would stand for a year before collapsing. This was a pure guess, but we were anxious not to shorten this time, and did not care if the time extended to two years, because we thought we would be well away from the area by then.

Of course, no one could expect prisoners of war to know anything about building houses and it was the German's job to oversee all the details. However, it was typical that the German was so wrapped up in his work that he expected everyone else to be as conscientious, especially if they made a great show of enjoying and being interested in the work as we did.

One day, in November 1944, we were all herded together and told that all prisoners of war were being sent back to Germany, but that the tradesmen were going now, and all those who had been doing bricklaying would be the first to go.

Consequently, we were given about twelve hours to organize our kit for marching and were to leave at six o'clock the next morning.

It was not light until about 8 am but about fifty of us had to march into Graudenz proper to join a further group of about a hundred and fifty.

When we were all assembled we started off at a good pace because this was the only way to keep warm, and we thought we were going to a railway station or to some form of transport, but after we had walked about twenty kilometres we realized that we were expected to walk the whole way.

That night we slept on straw in an old barn. The German bread was frozen so hard that it could not be cut with a knife, and the ersatz butter fragmented when we tried to cut it, so the only way to eat was to break them up by smashing them against a wooden beam, then putting a bit of bread and a bit of butter in the mouth to thaw out until it could be chewed and swallowed.

There was nothing else except the Red Cross food we carried with us, and that was not going to last for very long, so that night I decided that, if I were to survive, I would have to get away.

It was a lot easier than one would have thought because everyone was dog-tired, including the German guards, who were much older than we were and were not considered fit enough to fight on the Eastern Front because of age, war wounds or general unfitness. They really did have to be unfit because the army was accepting fifteen-year-old boys officially, which meant that some of the new recruits were as young as twelve years; the Wehrmacht was desperate for numbers to replace the huge losses on the Eastern Front. Also the 'People's Army', equivalent to the Home Guard in Britain, was composed of almost everyone considered unfit for the army, so it's easy to see that those guards in charge of the prisoners of war were really the dregs of the German army who, that night, were sleeping as soundly as anyone; and it had never entered anyone's head to post any night guards; none of them was fit enough to stay awake night and day.

In any case, only a madman would give up the warmth and coziness of the straw barn for the snow-covered freezing countryside with a strong icy wind blowing from the east from the vast plateau of Russia.

It was easy to put about three miles between me and the barn, and then I spent the rest of the night huddled up inside an old derelict shed which was almost completely covered in snow and was not too cold. The next day was trickier because I had constantly to duck out of the way if anyone was coming; fortunately, there was not too much traffic and one could see for no more than twenty or thirty yards at a time through the falling snow, and voices, clatter and other sounds were heard before anything was seen.

Eventually, I came to a familiar house where some old Polish people lived, who had a son in the Underground, who knew me by sight and could be trusted. They put me up for two days, in hiding, while they contacted someone else in the Underground. Although I didn't know this one, I trusted the old folks enough to trust him, and we had a long talk about what I should do.

General opinion was that the Russians were advancing and could overrun this area in three or four months. Most of the Poles were terrified of the Russians who, they said, were much less civilized than the Germans, and would rape all the women, kill many of the men, rob and pillage, as much as they liked. I was sure that this was an exaggeration, but had also heard that the Russian front-line troops had very little discipline and certainly raped any women to whom they took a fancy.

The Pole said that he and his companions wanted to be overrun by the Western Allies and would consider moving towards the German border.

Apparently, their general plan was to engage in a campaign aimed at slowing up the German retreat by blowing up certain bridges; they were at present engaged in placing charges under the long bridge over the Vistula at Torun.

Eventually, they agreed to help me to get back towards the German border, on the condition that I would assist them in mining the bridge. To this, I agreed.

There were no guards at the bridge and the Germans had

apparently never had any worries about the continuing integrity of the bridge because, apart from being as old as the hills, it was an integral part of the life of the town and was used by everyone, Poles and Germans alike.

Blowing up this bridge would be like blowing up a Town Hall or a Cathedral, something that seemed senseless on the face of it.

Anyway I am quite sure that, at this stage, the Germans had not considered the value of the bridge in a hurried retreat; or maybe the field officers had not considered the possibility of a hurried retreat, because no steps had been taken to guard the bridge.

The Polish opinion was that, if it were to be mined now, a constant watch could be kept on it, and if the German engineers started to look for charges, then it would be blown up at once from three distinct and separate sources.

So the Torun bridge was not difficult to approach and it was not all that difficult to slip under it to plant charges.

The construction was of timber on massive stone piles, with the weakest point midway between the piles. It was decided to place plastic charges along the main beams in sufficient quantities to blast these beams away.

The superstructure on the beams would then give way and the areas between the piles would fall into the fast-flowing Vistula.

It would take about a week for engineers to reconstruct the bridge and the Underground could also make sure that supplies for the reconstruction would be slowed up or stopped.

Fortunately for me, as it turned out, I had the section nearest to the bank to place charges and we did this at night over three nights, with a look-out at either end, and each of us had a section of the bridge between the piers.

By the third night, I had made good progress and was at the stage of connecting up the final wire lead which involved just twisting together two wires.

It was bitterly cold and my hands were numbed so that I

had to lock my arms around a beam in order to have my hands free, and my legs around another beam to stay in place while I used two hands to make the connection. I had just finished and was moving my cramped limbs preparatory to climbing back on to the surface of the bridge when I slipped on the icy timber and felt myself falling into the river.

It was a distance of about ten feet to the water, pitch black, icy cold and the Vistula had the reputation of being one of the fastest, if not the fastest-flowing river in the world and never gave up its dead.

I remember distinctly these thoughts flashing through my mind as I fell.

The next moment I hit the water with a huge shock and a big splash, and the icy waters closed over my head. I couldn't swim a stroke and was completely winded and disorientated.

I suppose that I must have struggled for a bit, probably threshed the water, but what happened, so I was told later, was that a current eddy had washed me near enough to the bank to allow the look-out, who had heard the splash, to pull me on to the bank, where he rubbed my face and hands with snow to warm me up and then, when I was sufficiently recovered, we made our way back to our house where I stripped, dried out and warmed up. I was helped by a drink of schnapps to stop my teeth chattering, and was no worse for the experience but counted myself extremely lucky.

Anyway I had done the best I could and was certainly in line for some transport west.

We discussed the best way to go and it was decided that I would travel to Poznan and then try to get the railway to Stettin.

From Stettin, travelling west-southwest would be simple because the emphasis of the German Railway Police was to search for people travelling north towards the coast, and they took little interest in people going towards the towns of Hamburg and even Bremen.

Finally, the Polish Underground came up with my travel

documents which simply described me as a carpenter from Konigsberg. I had a German name like so many of the Poles living in Danzig, and I was in a reserve occupation only as long as I had work. I had a work permit for a barrack complex being built at Sanbostel, a tiny village southwest of Hamburg, which was presumably going to house some of the troops returning from the Eastern Front. Anyway, it was a Wehrmacht project and my papers were stamped accordingly and were the best papers I'd had so far, so I felt reasonably secure on this count.

The only form of transport by rail for us was my old friend the cattle truck, but this time we were not overcrowded nor locked in and there were only about a dozen people in my truck. It had some straw in it so we were able to sit on the floor and lean against the sides of the railway wagon.

Because of the cold, we had the sliding door closed, and when we wanted to go to the toilet we either waited till the train stopped, which it did frequently, and then nipped out, keeping a very careful watch out for any signs of starting so that we were not caught with our trousers down, so to speak.

Otherwise, if the train was not going to stop and we could not wait, we poked our hind quarters out of the door and put up with the icy blast up our backside as well as the good-natured jokes of our travelling companions.

The fellow travellers were all country people, mostly travelling to see relatives, and all but three were men. There were two women and one girl of about ten, and they kept to the front end of the wagon whilst the rest of us formed a group at the rear end where we smoked cigarettes without inconveniencing the women.

The cigarettes I had were Polish, called Junak, which, like the Russian variety, had about an inch and a half of tobacco and two inches of cardboard tubing, which one pinched flat in two ways to produce a rough sort of filter or baffle so that the smoke cooled slightly before entering the mouth. This was just as well because these cigarettes had very strong tobacco indeed and took a bit of getting used to. The first time I smoked one, I spent about five minutes choking with a throat spasm.

We all had our own bread and sausage and the inevitable bottle of water, tea, coffee or even schnapps, although the latter was not my drink at all; I simply had water which I could refill at any time from a tap or even from the snow.

I had civilian clothes that were just warm enough and a warm thigh-length jacket which was enough to stop me getting really cold.

The train journey was seemingly endless because the trucks had a low priority and kept being shunted into sidings for an hour at a time.

The man sitting opposite me was a German train driver travelling to Hamburg. He was a very chatty bloke who spent most of the time talking; I think he liked to hear the sound of his own voice.

He was quite large, tall and very fat and wore thick padded trousers and matching overcoat and a very greasy blue railway cap which he used for wiping his nose or his hands or his face generally. He had a stubbly chin with beefy red cheeks and, when he wasn't talking, he was eating, and most of the time he was doing both, being careless about keeping his mouth shut so that whilst he talked and ate he sprayed around quite a bit of the food from his mouth.

Since he was sitting opposite me, he directed most of his conversation (and sprayed-out food) in my direction and I was hard pressed to keep my conversation to a minimum. I think I must have given him the impression that I was a pretty surly sort of customer, but he obviously had a very tough hide and didn't seem to lessen his conversation, punctuating his words with most of his sentences ending in '*nicht war?*' (not so?), which he used much as we would use 'eh?' This would be followed mostly by a rumbling laugh which exploded more half-chewed food in my direction. Fortunately the range was too great for him to score any direct hits.

We came to another series of shuddering halts and someone asked where we were and the fat man opposite said, almost without pausing in his narrative, that we were on the outskirts of Stettin. How he knew I don't know but one of the other men looked out of the little opening high up on the side of the truck and confirmed that we were indeed coming in to Stettin station.

I was looking forward to stretching my legs and having a break from my chatty opposite number, but the train just kept going and we passed right through the main station without even slowing. When eventually we did slow down, we went into a siding and stopped.

Only then, did we hear the strident sounds of the wailing air-raid sirens and distant shouts from the station, which was about a hundred yards back along the tracks. It was late afternoon and the light was poor and there was a cold mist drifting around the trucks.

All we could do was to close the sliding door again and go back to our places and wait for the all clear.

The fat train driver was completely unmoved by everything. He and I were discussing the use of self-coupling skips driven by a small diesel train, and I was quite interested in what he was telling me, because earlier I had a job of driving a small diesel train but we had not had any self-coupling skips, and he was describing the couplings when the first bombs dropped on the station.

With hardly a pause in his sentence, he listened to the sound of the planes and declared that they were Russian fighter bombers, and the next moment he was back on the subject of the skip couplings, and was diving into his large haversack to get out another load of food.

He had a small knife and he used this skilfully to cut a piece of bread, then a piece of wurst and then speared them on the point of the knife and conveyed them to his mouth, amidst the shattering sounds of explosions all round us, and, at the same time, he managed to carry on a conversation and to spray out food.

It was a performance that fascinated me to the extent that

my fear of the bombs was almost completely sublimated by his unconcern.

I thought that he had overdone things when he choked on a mouthful of food just when a particularly loud bang occurred which rocked the wagon, and I could see the look of seeming surprise on his face when he stopped chewing and stopped talking in the middle of a sentence.

One of the others had been hit in the leg with some fragments from the last bomb and was yelling with pain.

I had heard some whistling fragments come through the walls of the wagon and now I saw that there were quite a few holes in the wall.

At that moment a whole lot of splinters appeared in the roof overhead and the floor reflected this with more splinters kicking up about a yard from my feet and in a line down the centre of the wagon.

We were being machine-gunned by the planes and there was nothing to do except to make myself as small as possible by rolling up into the foetal position which is very comforting in times of crisis.

Finally, after what seemed like a very long time but was probably only a few minutes, we were aware that the sounds of the planes and the explosions had stopped and we were able to look around and see what damage had been done.

Our fat train driver was silent for once and he looked to be in a state of shock because he was poised with a piece of wurst on the point of his knife and his hand resting on his knee and his mouth slightly open.

"Are you alright?" I said to him, but he just sat there saying nothing.

I went over to him and shook his shoulder. He fell over sideways so that I could see the large hole in his back and the similar hole in the wagon side where a large steel bomb fragment had ripped through the timber wall and through his spine into the chest cavity, killing him instantly. In fact, he probably never felt anything hit him.

Two of the others were wounded and the man with the leg

wound looked pretty bad, so we opened the wagon door and one of the others went for help, whilst I ascertained that the rest were uninjured. The women were very brave but the little girl was crying and wailing and was probably in a state of shock.

I said that I would go and see if there were other casualties and I slipped out of the wagon and walked away in the snow towards the station.

The last thing I wanted was to be questioned by some official about the bombing raid and I decided that I would make my own way towards Hamburg, but I had to get some food from the station, and now was a good time to get some while there was a great deal of confusion.

The main part of the station was still intact, but further down a locomotive was lying almost across the line on its side and numerous troops were struggling with equipment and guns which had obviously formed part of a troop train and I expect that this was the cause of the intensive bombing raid.

The station area was nearly deserted and I was able to buy bread and sausage at the canteen in the station, without question, because these were the main two items that were in reasonably good supply and unrationed outside the cities and big industrial areas.

The women in the canteen were talking to each other nineteen to the dozen and paid scant attention to me as I made my purchases but just served me automatically.

I would have preferred a bicycle, but with the roads so snowbound I would probably be able to make more progress on foot, or so I thought. With a mental picture of the layout of the town, I struck off in a westerly direction, following the railway line going to Neustrelitz, where there was a large rail junction and the chance of a train to Hamburg.

By now it was getting dark and very cold. Too cold to snow, I thought, which was just as well because at this time of year even the railway lines would become covered with snow, making walking well nigh impossible in the dark as there would be no reflection from the metal lines.

I walked until I could go no further, probably for about four or five hours and then found a spot in which to sleep by the railway. It was an old shed which I suppose was railway property but had not been used for years by the look of it and it was ideal to sleep in.

It would have been about eight o'clock, I estimated, since it was just getting light, when I started off again after a brief meal. I replenished my bottle by scooping snow into it every few minutes until it was full of water. I was very careful not to eat the snow because this caused stomach cramps after a while due to the cold.

I spent nearly a week on this journey and made a routine of everything so that I kept going almost automatically.

Each morning I would rub my face with snow until it was glowing warm, and then I would carefully rub my precious piece of soap over the very light beard area; fortunately I had very little beard to shave, but it was a fetish with me to shave each morning and I had a German safety razor and two spare blades. Having shaved, I would have a bite to eat, and then set off on the march.

Sometimes I would walk along the middle of the road, if there had been no recent falls of snow, so that I didn't leave any tell-tale fresh footprints for anyone to notice. If it was snowing reasonably heavily, it would not matter too much, because the footprints would be covered over fairly quickly.

It was certainly easier to make progress on the highway, and the snow made everything so quiet and muffled that it was easy to hear a vehicle approaching from a distance, giving one plenty of time to hide.

Sleeping was often a problem, but under a hedge in a hollowed-out area was quite surprisingly warm and dry, especially if the snow was soft and fluffy, because at night it was too cold to melt and it was possible to sleep for short periods, especially as I was mostly dog-tired.

Food was also a problem and sometimes I was reduced to chewing charred wood; if I found a raw potato I would eat that, even though I knew it would make my mouth sore and dry.

Some days I just went without any food, even though I had a small part of my loaf untouched.

I was really filthy dirty except for outward appearances and these were all that mattered.

In the end I did not get to Neustrelitz but managed to hop on to a railway truck going in the general direction of Hamburg and was able to clean up a bit and not smell quite so bad.

I was a bit concerned over the numbness of my toes, especially the left foot, but I rubbed them with snow frequently and they were not too bad.

I was glad to be in the wagon, though, because it was very bitterly cold and the little bit of bread was not only stale but actually frozen; and though this may have stopped it going mouldy, it made it very difficult to eat because I had to chip off a bit and then suck it in my mouth before it was soft enough to chew.

By the time I reached the southern outskirts of Hamburg, as I thought, I was really in a bad way and I was getting to the stage when I was prepared to take a few risks to get food and a wash.

I decided to get off the wagon and go on into Hamburg on foot and just play it by ear since it was certain that I could not last very much longer. My left toes were beginning to ache and I was walking with a limp.

I limped along for about an hour when I heard voices and moved cautiously towards them.

There were two men leaning on shovels who had been clearing the snow away from the entrance to some sort of electrical substation, probably a transformer station. There were a number of these that I had passed.

As I got nearer, I realized that the men were speaking French and I could see that they were wearing very old and worn French Army greatcoats. They also had fur hats with ear flaps tying under their chins, instead of the more usual ear pads and cap such as I was wearing.

I went up to them and said: "*Bonjour, Messieurs, excusez-moi, mais est ce que vous êtes prisonniers de guerre?*" (Good day, gentlemen, excuse me but are you prisoners of war?)

They looked at me suspiciously and one replied: "*Et alors?*" (So what?)

I told them that I was an escaped British prisoner of war and that I needed some help.

They were a bit cautious at first, asking me in bad English to say where in England I came from, so I told them in English that I lived in London but had been taken prisoner in Calais.

Their attitude changed dramatically and they said that they were a small working party on parole and that they could help me back to their quarters to clean up and get some food.

Apparently I had struck it lucky because they were paroled workers who had simply undertaken to do work in Germany on the understanding that they would not try to escape, and they were not guarded, but were subject to checks by the local police.

There were only six of them and they assured me that they were all loyal Frenchmen who detested the Boche and were only too pleased to help me.

So they took me back to their house, which was clean as a whistle and very tidy, and I was able to have a bath, the first since I had left Herr Staub's farm, and I had a hot soup and felt really happy.

They said that I could sleep there in an alcove which could be a hiding place if the police came.

The only fly in the ointment was that when I got into the bath I found that the toes of my left foot were black with gangrene and stank to high heaven. They were also extremely painful and I realized that they were frostbitten and that I was going to lose them.

I had all sorts of horrible ideas that the gangrene would creep up my foot and poison my system or at least make my foot drop off, but one of the Frenchmen knew about first aid and had seen frostbite before; he told me that I would just lose the toes.

It turned out not to be so bad, because I only lost half of two toes and a third of two more.

The pain during this time was all-consuming, and I think I must have been a bit delirious because I have fleeting memories of Raoul, the first-aid Frenchman, dressing my foot twice daily, which felt as if he were tearing the ends of the toes off, and sprinkling the toes with Iodoform powder which reduced the stink of the gangrene. I can remember that I drew my feet in, if anyone came within two yards of me, because I was afraid of someone kicking against the toes.

Chapter 10

1945

From time to time during this episode, a number of other Frenchmen came along to the house, and I was fairly apprehensive about the open way the French displayed me like some exhibit. I felt that it would only need some unwise word and I could be the centre of unwanted attention by the German Police.

When I hesitatingly asked Georges, one of the original Frenchmen, about this, he first of all burst out laughing, and then shrugged his shoulders in true Gallic fashion and said that all the Frenchmen were loyal supporters of Le Grand Charles (Charles De Gaulle) and could be trusted not to collaborate. "In fact," he said with a laugh "one or two of these friends are in the Underground."

I was quite astonished by this and tried to think of ways to gain their confidence enough to let me join them.

As my foot got better, they talked about ways of getting me out of Germany. By degrees, I convinced them that it was my job to remain in Germany as long as possible, and to help them as much as I could, and as much as they would allow me.

I met quite a few of them after this, and I was inclined to

think they trusted me after one of their number, who spoke fluent English, had a long conversation with me which was all one-sided, in that he learned all about me, but I found out nothing about him, not even his name.

Eventually, I was accepted and was told that the main objective was to sabotage railways and vehicles, especially in the regions to and from Hamburg and Bremen, which were the principal towns in this area.

They told me there was a large concentration camp at Buchholz and that the barracks where I was to have worked at Sanbostel were, in reality, old forts which were to be converted to concentration camps, and already a large number of Jews and German dissidents were imprisoned there.

I also learned that the Germans were moving the bulk of their Allied prisoners of war into this region so that the inevitable bombing of the large cities would kill a large number of these prisoners.

Whether this was true or whether it was part of the wild propaganda that was constantly fed to all civilian personnel, I had no way of ascertaining, but it was a reasonable bet that the prisoner of war camps would be known to the Allies and, as far as possible, would be avoided.

On the other hand, the blanket bombing by the Americans was not able to discriminate between small areas within their general targets for night bombing; generally these attacks were directed towards Kiel, in the north, and in the south, Hamburg, Bremen, and Berlin itself.

As my foot got better, I was very relieved to find that only the end joints of three toes were gone and though the blackness had involved the whole toes, it was only skin deep for half of them, so I was soon able to walk with very little limp and started to accompany the French members of the Underground.

At the same time, I reluctantly said goodbye to the friendly Frenchmen who had looked after me so well and went to live in a cheap little doss house on the outskirts of Luneburg, and my so good papers were skilfully altered to allow me to work in that area. This actually only required a rubber stamp in one of the corners and a scribbled signature over the stamp. This was unlikely to be found out, since, as I had discovered on many occasions, the German mentality had a great faith in papers and documents and all things official, and thus seldom suspected any convincing-looking document.

By the same token, if a German came and started giving orders, it was surprising how often the mention of superiors would deflate and divert them.

When we went out on a sabotage job, it was almost always at night and we were armed against a surprise meeting with the Germans, whether Police or Military we were determined not to be caught, and, if discovered, we were to shoot it out and try to get away as best we could. Thank goodness that my group never had to use their weapons, because this was in the middle of Germany and, although the bulk of the male population was away at war, there were still a significant number of able-bodied Germans to look after the home front.

I had a Polish Radom automatic which delivered a nine-millimetre punch with fair accuracy but a great deal of noise. This was unsuitable for taking a silencer, so any time I had to use it, I would be advertising the fact over a great distance. Nevertheless, it was a great comfort to have something with which to defend myself should the occasion arise.

I used to keep my weapon under a loose floor board near my bed so that it was readily available at short notice. Later I got into the habit of keeping it under my pillow and it acted like a security blanket, I suppose, because I never had any problems about sleeping and would awake only if I heard some unusual noise in the night.

The daytime work we did was extremely light and certainly not very demanding. We were employed by the local council to do mostly maintainance, odd digging work and carpentry repair work. I had to admire the way the Frenchmen had organized themselves; it almost appeared as if they were the employers instead of the Germans. They seemed to determine what work was done, and where, and the German bosses just agreed and let them get on with it.

So we harried and worried the rail and road services around the Hamburg area, never openly attacking but always seeking a covert solution which, if possible, would or could be attributed to mechanical failure.

A rivet jamming points and a short obliterating the green light on a railway, long-fuse explosives on departing trains, long-fuse incendiaries in the coal tenders, loose railway lines with no spikes holding the rail were extremely difficult to spot and, if done on the outside rail on the outer arc of a fast curving stretch of track, were pretty lethal.

Vehicles were generally easier to sabotage because they were nearly all heavy army vehicles driven by relatively unskilled personnel, the original drivers having been transferred to active service, and the general maintainance on the lorries was very poor so that they were tending to break down frequently anyway.

With a hacksaw blade, a handful of sand, a bit of grease and a bit of know-how, one could render lorries helpless in a variety of ways which were difficult to detect. The Germans, at this stage of the war, simply did not have the people to look after their transport.

It was a question of not if but when Germany was going to lose the war, and this was the attitude of the majority of Germans, although they would certainly not voice this opinion openly.

All that the civilians were concerned with was that British, French or American troops should be the ones to overrun them and not the Russians who, with a dreadful reputation for revenge and rape, would understandably be thinking of the German *Blitzkrieg* against their Mother Russia; the Russian troops had no knowledge of the Geneva Convention where Germans were concerned.

I would think that this feeling was not really justified but it would have been difficult to convince the German civilians otherwise.

At this time, too, the defence of Germany was in the hands of truly fanatical Nazis of all ages. Particularly in the *Hitler Jugend*, the Hitler Youth Movement, there were young boys of ten to fifteen years of age whose whole life had been dedicated to the Fuehrer, as their God, and who were willing to die for him and determined to inflict as much damage, and to kill as many of his enemies, as possible, before they themselves were killed. These youngsters were not going to be captured alive, if they could help it.

They were the children who had been recruited into the Hitler Jugend at an early age, whether they were willing or not, and they were told that Germany's future was in their hands.

They were encouraged to report their own parents to the Gestapo for trivial things like getting extra food on the Black Market for their family, or expressing doubts within the family that Hitler was anything but perfect.

They seemed to be everywhere and the younger they were the more deadly their hatred of all things anti-Hitler.

They went out of their way to follow anyone they suspected, and the Gestapo encouraged them; the fact of guilt at this time was relatively unimportant, and fear was the weapon used by the Gestapo to drive the German people on, even in the face of certain destruction. Anyone suspected of subversive activity, be it by word of mouth, or even by failure to salute the Fuehrer enthusiastically, would be under suspicion and would probably merit detention in a labour or concentration camp.

The German population thus began to assume a permanently hunted and cautious mien that said more for the failure of the war effort than all the news from the Front, news which seemed to be uniformly of one kind, namely that so and so had died in heavy fighting on the Eastern Front.

The 'Volkischer Beobachter', which was the popular newspaper in our area, consisted mainly of front-page news of advances against the Allies, which no one really believed, and pages devoted to lists of those dearly loved uncles, brothers, fathers and sons who had died gloriously for Fuehrer and Fatherland, which everyone believed.

Early in 1945 the bombing of Hamburg intensified and nightly raids were common and quite terrifying.

Although I was often ten to fifteen kilometres away from the bombed areas, the ground shifted about half a metre underfoot, or so it seemed, so that it was difficult to stand without overbalancing, and the whole effect was like an earthquake, with constant lightning and thunder but with the addition of ground movement and blasts of ear-splitting proportions. The bombs dropped were called blockbusters by both sides and they had the effect of just that.

It was difficult to imagine that anyone or anything could survive such a pasting, yet the next morning things seemed to be going on as usual except for big gaps of rubble where three or four buildings had just disintegrated into dust and broken bricks, with little possibility of the passage of cars or even bicycles.

Pedestrians picked their tortuous way cautiously over the rubble on their way to work. There were also groups, mostly old women and children, wearily searching the rubble for any signs of their belongings or even their relatives and friends.

There was no triumph or satisfaction in my heart over these horrible raids, and I felt a deep sympathy for all those innocent people who had suffered this senseless destruction in their towns.

I realized that it was necessary to convince the enemy that war was not just giving it to the other side but also taking it. I thought of the news broadcasts that I had heard about the bombing of London and the big cities of England and this served to take the edge off any feeling of shame I had about such mass destruction of German towns.

It was in March 1945 that we turned our attention to the concentration camps in the area of Buchholz, Horsfeld and Bremevorde.

We knew that the Allies were driving in that direction and we were anxious to bring some hope and relief to the poor souls who were dying in these camps.

We were not equipped to force our way in and kill all the

guards, nor did we have the numbers for any direct assault. However, we had a large quantity of explosives and we could get to the perimeters of the camps at night without being detected. There were guards but no dogs as far as we could find out, and a night operation seemed the best approach.

We planned to blow up areas in these three camps simultaneously at night. If we were lucky, we might time things to coincide with the nightly air raids and this would allow us to attack again the next night and so on.

Two Frenchmen and I had the camp at Bremevorde, which was furthest west, nearer the Allied approach but furthest from Hamburg and the air raids.

We did a few preliminary reconnaissances and decided that the best sites to blow were the guardhouse and four towers. This way, although not at random as with an errant pilot just dropping his bombs anywhere, we stood to knock out the German guard population with least possibility of involving the prisoners.

There were British, French, Polish, Russian, German and American prisoners in this camp and also a number of 'stripeys' who could have been any nationality but were almost certain to be Jews, because they were the worst nourished and had been in the camp for the longest time.

One of our Frenchmen had actually been in the camp as an electrician and odd job man and he had a good idea of the general layout of the various compounds.

This camp was not arranged like the other ones I had seen, which were roughly square. This was elongated with the guardhouse outside the entrance, and a guardroom inside the compound, and then a long road through the middle of the camp with huts and bunkers on either side.

The barbed wire along the perimeter was excessive and arranged with a fire corridor so that no one could escape that way.

The bunkers were interesting in that they had strong concrete sloping entrances, the walls of which were about a foot and a half thick; they looked as if they had been built a long time before the rest of the camp.

The prisoners seemed to be able to mix, except for the 'stripeys' who were in a compound within a compound, and well ringed with barbed wire. Even so, the relatively well-off prisoners of war were able to pass food and cigarettes to the concentration area, which was why the 'stripeys' spent all day waiting by the wire for food.

There were men and women in this concentration area, and they were all dressed alike in trousers and loose-fitting shirts which reached down to their mid-thighs, for the most part; although I think they were all the same size, and if you were short they came down low, and if you were tall they only reached to the waist.

It was difficult to tell the women from the men because they all had their heads shaved every week to keep down the lice population, and they mostly wore little pill-box hats covering the shorn areas. All their garments and hats were uniformly made of coarse grey material with vertical stripes of blue or black about an inch wide.

The far end of the camp was guarded by two tall towers that housed four guards each, with one from each group patrolling the outside of the wire, and the others constantly traversing the machine guns, as if they expected a mass breakout at any moment.

The Frenchman who had been in the camp said that the reason they were so keen was that they themselves were scrutinized by the Feldwebel, and if they were seen to be slack, they were reported and shipped off to the Front.

I have no doubt that the Feldwebel, in turn, was watched by his superiors and so on, because that's how the system worked.

We decided that we would place six charges, two at the main entrance by the Kommandant's quarters where the guards had their sleeping areas, and one at each tower on each corner of the camp.

The main gate was easy because one could, with no

difficulty, creep up to the back of the building, under cover of darkness, and plant the charges; but the two towers at the far end were a real puzzle.

They were built on the corner of the camp in such a way that they could cover the fire corridors along the borders of the barbed wire; that is, they had a fire traverse of slightly more than ninety degrees.

A very good thing, from our point of view, was that the remaining two sides of the square look-out at the top of the tower was boarded in so that the wind, rain and snow did not sweep through the look-out post. This meant that the guards in the tower could not see anything away from the camp, and this, in turn, meant that the two towers had a common blind spot. Had it not been so, we would always have been under the eye of one or other of the guards in the towers. Also, at night, the guards were reduced to two per tower and they did not patrol the corridors at all, and the camp lights were, for the most part, illuminating the area of the wire fencing and did not illuminate the towers, so that the area immediately at the back of the towers was in the shadows.

So, one night, we approached the towers from the back area and were able to place fused charges at the base of each tower and retreat safely. The fuses were mechanically timed and set for four hours on each tower charge, so that they would go off all together at ten pm, which was the time that the night bombing got under way.

We retreated all the way back to our work hut where we often spent the night safely away from the bombs.

Sure enough, at a few minutes before ten, the sirens started wailing and the distant ack-ack guns started their nightly chorus whilst searchlights swept the skies, occasionally settling on a bomber and making it look like a tiny fairy light in the sky.

Shortly after this the parachute flares started to fall, like huge candelabras, lighting up the terrain almost like a sunrise, but with a great deal of smoke.

Then the bombs started falling and we felt the now familiar

rocking back and forth of the ground and the thunderous explosions tearing into Hamburg.

Hundreds of planes were involved, some sweeping near to the ground with smoke trailing from them disappearing over the horizon to the west. The majority of the planes, however, remained high in the sky and in rigid formation, with little puff-balls of smoke from the anti-aircraft shells dotting the sky all around and below them, beautifully lit up by the searchlights.

It was certainly an awe-inspiring sight, once seen never to be forgotten. It was difficult to imagine that hundreds of people were being killed in the cities being bombed that night.

It was a large raid and lasted about half-an-hour.

Finally the sirens sounded again with a steady note as the noise of the guns faded into the distance, and the sky remained crimson with the fires raging in the city.

It had been so enthralling that we had forgotten all about our own little display which was puny in the extreme by comparison, and we were professional enough not to go and see what damage we had inflicted. On the contrary, we determined to stay away until the following night when we would place more charges and vary the sites.

So the next night we returned to the camp site to inspect the damage and to place fresh charges.

We proceeded very cautiously, in case there was an ambush, approaching the camp site from the back end where the rear two towers were.

Or rather where the towers had been, because they were both down, lying forlornly on their sides, with no guards in sight.

We worked our way round to the front of the camp and, sure enough, the Kommandantura was completely demolished and deserted.

We figured that the Germans would not leave the prisoners unguarded so they must be inside the camp. There were no lights at all showing and we suspected a trap so we hurriedly withdrew and went back to our work shed without laying any more charges.

We decided that we would come back in the morning light and see what had happened.

So at about 8.30 am the next morning, carrying shovels and our work bags, we went into the area surrounding the camp; the plan was to set up some surveyor poles and start digging a hole, if anyone queried our presence.

However, when we got to the camp entrance there was still no sign of any of the Germans, not even any dead ones, so we went up to the main gate with our survey poles and shovels to find out where the guards were.

Much to our astonishment, we found that the gates were no longer padlocked and we were able to open them and go into the compound. We were now inside the camp and only separated from the prisoners by a secondary gate.

There were a few prisoners around watching us idly and probably wondering what we were up to.

We asked in French where the guards were and the prisoners we spoke to didn't understand us, so we made signs asking for anyone who could speak French or German, and eventually came across an American Corporal who could speak some German, and we asked him where the guards were.

He said they were all outside the camp in the main guardhouse, and he was quite unbelieving when we said that there was no one there and only a bombed out shell of the guardhouse remaining.

We coaxed him to the entrance and finally managed to convince him that the place was not only deserted but mostly demolished. Presumably there had been so much noise and commotion that the prisoners had not been aware of any of the camp damage.

He went at a trot back into the camp and came out with a Master Sergeant and we went through the same procedure.

It was quite entertaining to see the look on the Sergeant's face; one could almost see him swell up as he regained his lost authority.

He strode back into the camp and yelled with a stentorian voice: "Hey, Littlejohn, tell the guys the Krauts have gone."

An incredibly thin, tall wisp of a young man came out of one of the huts and dreamily looked in our direction and said in a really cissy voice: "George, I really thought you said the Kraut guards had gone."

The Sergeant said, very patiently, I thought: "Littlejohn, you get your G.I. butt back there through that door and go tell the guys to get the hell out here, d'you hear."

The Sergeant then turned round to us and said to the German-speaking Corporal: "Ask these guys who they are and what they're doing."

Before the Corporal could reply I said: "That won't be necessary. We're members of the French Resistance and we are just as surprised as you to find that the guards have left."

"You speak good English." Slightly suspiciously.

"I should speak good English, I am English." I replied.

It was obviously the Sergeant's day for surprises because for once he was fairly speechless. Muttering 'a goddammed Limey and goddammed Frogs' under his breath, he solemnly shook each of us by the hand and invited us into the hut.

It was interesting to see the amounts of food and cigarettes scattered around the place.

We were offered D-bars of slab chocolate, cartons of Lucky Strike and Chesterfield cigarettes and tins of 100% All-Coffee.

By the time we had eaten some C-ration crackers and Spam and thanked them for their hospitality, the news had spread through the camp like wildfire, and the camp entrance was filled with excited prisoners of war.

The Master Sergeant appeared to have some authority and I advised him that the situation outside was unknown, and that anyone just walking out of the camp was taking a chance of being shot at, and that the best thing they could do was to organize themselves to leave the camp after about twenty-four hours, by which time we could try to find out what the situation was.

It was now about noon and we felt that we should get out of the way in case the Germans came back, and, indeed, we had been hearing both artillery and mortar fire and had persuaded the prisoners that the best place at this time was in the bunkers of the camp.

It was impossible to tell the direction from which they came, but fairly certainly they were not aiming for the camp, because the canvas-ripping sound was passing well overhead and we were just getting a few of the shortfall shells.

After about twenty minutes they stopped, and there was an eerie silence.

Then first one and then another of us heard it.

Uncertain what it was at first, after a few minutes of the sound coming and going, we could hear the low, muttering growl which increased and decreased as the wind caught the sound and tossed it about.

As the minutes went by the sound increased and it was apparent that a large number of tanks were approaching.

Tantalizingly, we could not tell from which direction they were coming. One moment you could swear it was from the east and the next from the north and so on, but the noise grew louder and louder and suddenly someone yelled something and we saw no fewer than six tanks, great big lumbering dusty tanks, coming towards us from the north-west, with complete disregard for the roadways but approaching in a row about a hundred yards apart, with more tanks appearing over the distant crest, until it seemed that they were standing poised on the horizon and then swooping down towards us leaving little clouds of dust or exhaust behind them.

As they got nearer, we could see the little squadron flags, and some of the prisoners were shouting that they were British tanks, and then I could only see them in a blur as the tears started running down my face and all the pent-up emotion and frustration of the last long five years burst out.

They were indeed tanks of the Household Cavalry, the crack Guards Regiment, and, as they swept by, they had a reception from the prisoners that was spine-tingling; all the prisoners were yelling and screaming their heads off, and the

140

tank commanders were acknowledging this with waving hands as they went by.

I could not help thinking about that day, five years ago almost, when the crack Panzers of K Division had swept into Calais, all-conquering and as impressive as were the British tanks now.

The war for me had come a full circle and I was now seeing the final stages of Germany's defeat.

Half-an-hour after the tanks came the truckloads of infantry, just as impressive in their way, though not so spectacular.

They were very efficient and confident, very friendly and full of curiosity about our situation.

I had a chance to speak to a young lieutenant and he said that he would get some orders cracking to get me back to England for a debriefing. I did not know the term debriefing, which had been used by the British only in the latter part of the war as far as I knew. It sounded American, but I just nodded as if this was what I had expected, and said that I would be around if he needed me.

I settled down to sleep in the camp that night, but I might as well have tried to walk to the moon for all the sleep I got. I was so excited that I had to keep getting up to look out of the windows to make sure that this was real and not just another of the dreams that I had for many years of the war ending. I kept reminding myself that this was the end of the war for me, AND THAT I HAD SURVIVED when I had all the time lived from day to day in the certainty that I could not survive.

In the morning, the first of the German prisoners were herded into the camp, quite properly into the concentration camp area where the 'stripeys' had been, and, as they passed by the guardroom, they had to throw down any weapons they had been carrying. By the end of the morning there was a huge pile of rifles, pistols (mostly Lugers), bayonets, machine-pistols (mostly Schmeissers) and some of the dinky little 'dress' pistols worn by clerical officers who would never have used them anyway.

Throughout the morning, mortar shells had been falling and machine-gun fire sounded sporadically, and we were told that mostly the resistance was being provided by early teenage Hitler Jugend members who were determined to die for their Fuehrer.

It was fascinating to watch the mortar shells, which were quite visible from where we were; one could see the tiny black dot rise up into the sky, describe a graceful parabola, and then drop down to earth; it seemed quite a few seconds later that the dull crump of the explosion occurred.

At lunch-time, the lieutenant came to tell me that I was being taken out by truck to an Air Force forward base where I would be flown back to England.

I said an emotional goodbye to the Frenchmen and to my new G.I. companions, the G.I. standing for Government Issue, by the way, and went over to the truck which was waiting at the camp gate.

I was too excited to think of anything, other than getting out of Germany, as quickly as possible.

There were some other people in the truck, I noticed, as I climbed over the tailboard, and we straightaway set off westward.

It happened as we were crossing a small river only a mile from the camp.

There was a big explosion and the truck lurched sideways but continued over the bridge, accelerating furiously and bumping us around all over the floor of the truck where we had taken refuge.

Bits of shrapnel were ripping through the canvas sides of the truck as we all lay flat on the floor. I remember saying a quick prayer asking that it should not end here after all the narrow escapes I had survived, and really thinking that perhaps it was going to end like this anyway.

However, the driver kept going hell for leather along the road and eventually we were out of range and safe.

We swept into an open space where there was quite a sizeable runway and drove up to an old Dakota which was

142

ticking over on the tarmac. As soon as we were all aboard, the plane lumbered forward and with no effort at all lifted off the ground and turned westward.

We flew over Southern Holland and the pilot circled round Arnhem to show us the tangled remains of the gliders which had crashed there, and then we flew on to land at Brussels Airport.

We were to spend the night in Brussels and then to fly on in the morning. I had a really great night celebrating with some British, French and Belgian soldiers, but remember very little of that night because I got fairly drunk and spent the night with blankets on the floor of the cafe with some of the other soldiers.

In the morning I was collected and taken back to the aerodrome, where I boarded a Lancaster bomber with about twenty other people and we took off to fly to England.

I remember nothing of that flight except that it was extremely noisy, bumpy and uncomfortable sitting on the bare framework of the plane's floor, but it seemed to make the distance very quickly because we presently lost altitude and made a really soft landing on English soil.

We landed somewhere in Kent and, as I got off the plane, I had the most marvellous smell of cut English grass, lush and very green, the like of which exists nowhere else on earth.

It was two months short of five years since I had smelled that wonderful grass.